THE GREEK Al
HISTORIANS

The Classical World Series

Aristophanes and his Theatre of the Absurd, Paul Cartledge
Art and the Romans, Anne Haward
Athens and Sparta, S. Todd
Athens Under the Tyrants, J. Smith
Attic Orators, Michael Edwards
Augustan Rome, Andrew Wallace-Hadrill
Cicero and the End of the Roman Republic, Thomas Wiedemann
Classical Archaeology in the Field, S.J. Hill, L. Bowkett and K. & D. Wardle
Classical Epic: Homer and Virgil, Richard Jenkyns
Democracy in Classical Athens, Christopher Carey
Environment and the Classical World, Patricia Jeskins
Greece and the Persians, John Sharwood Smith
Greek and Roman Historians, Timothy E. Duff
Greek and Roman Medicine, Helen King
Greek Architecture, R. Tomlinson
Greek Tragedy: An Introduction, Marion Baldock
Julio-Claudian Emperors, Thomas Wiedemann
Lucretius and the Didactic Epic, Monica Gale
Morals and Values in Ancient Greece, John Ferguson
Mycenaean World, K. & D. Wardle
Plato's Republic and the Greek Enlightenment, Hugh Lawson-Tancred
Political Life in the City of Rome, J.R. Patterson
Religion and the Greeks, Robert Garland
Religion and the Romans, Ken Dowden
Roman Architecture, Martin Thorpe
Roman Britain, S.J. Hill and S. Ireland
Roman Satirists and Their Masks, Susanna Braund
Slavery in Classical Greece, N. Fisher
The Plays of Euripides, James Morwood
Women in Classical Athens, Sue Blundell

Classical World Series

THE
GREEK AND ROMAN
HISTORIANS

Timothy E. Duff

Bristol Classical Press

First published in 2003 by
Bristol Classical Press
an imprint of
Gerald Duckworth & Co. Ltd.
61 Frith Street, London W1D 3JL
Tel: 020 7434 4242
Fax: 020 7434 4420
inquiries@duckworth-publishers.co.uk
www.ducknet.co.uk

A catalogue record for this book is available
from the British Library

ISBN 1 85399 601 7

Printed and bound in Great Britain by
Antony Rowe Ltd, Chippenham, Wiltshire

Contents

List of illustrations   7
Abbreviations   8
Preface   9

1. Introduction   11
2. Herodotos   13
3. Thucydides   25
4. Fourth-century historians   39
5. Hellenistic historians   53
6. Roman Republican historians   63
7. Livy   79
8. Imperial Rome   90
9. Historians of imperial Rome: Tacitus   93
10. Historians of imperial Rome: other voices   102
11. Greek historians of the Roman imperial period   107

Epilogue   122

Suggestions for further study   123
Suggestions for further reading   126
Index   131

Για τους έλληνες φίλους μου

List of illustrations

Fig. 1 The periods of ancient history as traditionally conceived   10

Fig. 2 Map of Greece and the Aegean in the fifth and fourth
centuries BC   14

Fig. 3 Map of the Hellenistic world   54

Fig. 4 Map of the Roman world   62

Fig. 5 The Roman emperors   80

Fig. 6 Map of the Roman Empire, *c.* AD 120   108

Fig. 7 Chronological table showing historians and major events   120

Abbreviations

CIL   *Corpus Inscriptionum Latinarum* (Berlin 1896-).

D-K   H. Diels and W. Kranz, eds, *Die Fragmente der Vorsokratiker* (Berlin 1966).

FGrH   *Die Fragmente der griechischen Historiker* (ed. F. Jacoby, Berlin 1923-30; Leiden 1940-58).

IG   *Inscriptiones Graecae* (Berlin 1913-).

ILS   *Inscriptiones Latinae Selectae* (ed. H. Bessau, Berlin 1892-1914).

Migne   J.-P. Migne, ed., *Patrologia Latina* (Paris 1844-65).

ML   R. Meiggs and D.M. Lewis, eds, *A selection of Greek historical inscriptions to the end of the fifth century* BC (Oxford 1988).

Preface

This book was written in Athens, Kythera and Reading between Summer 2000 and Summer 2002. I am especially grateful to the British School at Athens and to Cyprian Broodbank of the Kythera Island Project for their hospitality, as well as to Bristol Classical Press for their patience. Vina Balaskas, Alastair Blanshard, Paul Cartledge, Jane Gardner, Vangelio Kiriatzi and Stephen Oakley gave up their time to read drafts. Diotima Papadi helped with some of the references. I am grateful to all, and especially to Vangelio Kiriatzi, who also produced the maps and tables. The mistakes that remain are, of course, entirely my own. Finally, my thanks to all those others without whose friendship and company over the last two years the writing of this book would have been a less pleasant task, including – but not limited to – Jill and Jeremy Duff, Taeko Goto, Angela Hadjivasiliou, Yuri Hara, Hwayong Lee, Andy and Vlatka Nercessian, Evdokia Michalopoulou, Pantelis Michelakis, Shant Nercessian, Spyridoula Varlokosta and Maria Xanthou.

All translations are my own, though I have consulted throughout the work of other translators and commentators. I have not been able to acknowledge in the text itself my debt to these and to the numerous scholars whose works I have used, summarised or discussed. I beg their indulgence and plead in my defence only the constraints of the genre in which I find myself writing. I have transliterated Greek names as precisely as possible, except in a few cases where I have placed the demands of familiarity above those of consistency (e.g. Thucydides, Oedipus).

Reading – Cambridge   T.E.D.
July 2002

c. 1600 – *c.* 1200 BC	Mycenaean Civilisation
c. 1200 – *c.* 800 BC	Dark Ages
c. 800 – 508 BC	Archaic Age
508 – 323 BC	Classical Age
323 – 31 BC	Hellenistic Age
31 BC – AD 324	Roman Period
AD 325 –	Late Antique or Early Byzantine Age

Fig. 1 The periods of ancient history as traditionally conceived

It is important to note that these names and dates are conventional only. In addition some scholars vary the starting and ending point of these periods slightly: thus, some think of the Classical period proper as beginning only after the Persian Wars in 479 BC, and some place the end of the Hellenistic world in 146 BC with the annexation of mainland Greece rather than in 31 BC with the fall of Ptolemaic Egypt. Furthermore, periodisation is almost always retrospective: to people living at the time such categories would have made little sense.

Chapter 1

Introduction

History for the ancient Greeks began with the *Iliad*, one of the epic poems ascribed to Homer. The *Iliad* is in fact the product of a long oral tradition stretching back over several hundreds of years; it was only finally committed to writing some time in the seventh century BC, after many generations of change and evolution. For the Greeks, however, Homer was a single poet, revered as the fountain-head of all literary genres. Some might have criticised his stories as implausible; they might have objected to the idea of the gods appearing on the human stage and intervening in earthly affairs. But in many ways the *Iliad* set the agenda for later Greek and Roman historians.

The *Iliad* concerns a great war, and describes the exploits of the heroes who fought in it. The scene is set before the walls of Troy, which the Greeks have been besieging for some unspecified time. A quarrel has broken out between Achilles, one of the Greek commanders, and Agamemnon 'Lord of Men', the leader of the Greek host:

> Sing, goddess, of the rage of Achilles, Peleus' son,
> doomed and murderous, that brought innumerable pains
> on the Achaians, pitched into Hades the brave souls
> of many heroes and made them prey for dogs
> and birds: the will of Zeus was being done.
> Begin when first the two men parted in their quarrel,
> Agamemnon, lord of men, and godlike Achilles.
> Which of the gods brought these two together to fight in strife?
> It was the son of Leto and Zeus …
>
> (*Iliad* 1.1-9)

The bloody events which follow upon this dispute are narrated in chronological sequence. Only in passing do we learn of the origin of the Greek attack on Troy ten years earlier: it was undertaken in order to recover Helen, wife of Agamemnon's brother, who had eloped with a Trojan prince, Paris. Interspersed with this narrative of battles and bloodshed are long speeches put into the mouths of the leading protagonists. The language of the *Iliad* is poetic and carefully chosen to fit the strict epic metre; the narrative is dramatic and moving. Above all, it was meant for entertainment, for recitation on festive occasions. It also has a strong moral and religious dimension: it shows a universe in which the brave are rewarded and the cowardly shamed; it not only narrates the quarrels and heroic clashes of the heroes, but relates them, as we see in the opening lines, to the will of the gods, as well as to justice and to fate. There is a tragic sense to the *Iliad* too. It certainly glorifies the heroic code of the protagonists, who put honour before life; but it also causes the reader to reflect on the tragedy of war, and of lost youth, and to sympathise with the defeated, be they Greek or Trojan.

It was another two centuries or so after the *Iliad* was written down before the first prose work of history was composed in Greek, that of Herodotos. But many of the elements present in the *Iliad* are to be found in varying degrees in his narratives, and in those of the Greek and Roman historians who followed. For them, Homer remained the ultimate model. Most strikingly, history never lost its essential association with war and politics, with the grand stage of human affairs; it was consequently never much interested in social life or economics, or in the affairs of women. It was meant, in addition, to be entertaining: expression and language were considered important, as was an exciting plot. Furthermore, the Greek and Roman historians would see their role not simply as narrating but as offering comment or reflection on the nature of the world, or as providing moral lessons for their readers. It may indeed seem surprising to us that history had its origins in epic poetry, in descriptions of the conflicts of men and gods. But this should act as a salutary reminder that, as we approach the ancient historians, we should do our best to put aside modern notions of what history should be, and rather look at how it developed within the societies of Greece and Rome. To do this, we turn to the earliest surviving Greek writer of prose narrative: Herodotos.

Chapter 2

Herodotos

Herodotos and Homer

Herodotos, like so many of the Greek intellectuals of the sixth and fifth centuries BC, was from the west coast of Asia Minor. He was born in the Greek city of Halikarnassos around 484 BC, when this area was still under Persian rule. The Persian Empire had two generations before taken control of the cities of Asia Minor. In 499 BC many of these coastal cities revolted from Persia. The war which followed, known to modern historians as the Ionian revolt, set in train a sequence of events which were to change the world. Most of the Greek cities of the mainland had avoided getting caught up in the conflict with Persia, but Athens and the small city of Eretria in Euboia sent a modest naval contingent to aid the insurgents. Thus it was that, after suppressing the revolt, the Persians launched an expeditionary force to punish these two cities. To the amazement of Greek and Persian alike, this force was defeated by the small Athenian army at the Battle of Marathon (490 BC). Ten years later a massive invasion of mainland Greece proper began. This time the Persians came with much larger numbers. They broke through the Greek defences at Thermopylai and sacked Athens. But this invasion too was, incredibly, defeated by the combined forces of Athens, Sparta and Sparta's Peloponnesian allies at the battles of Salamis, Plataia and Mykale (480-479 BC). Athens went on to expel the Persians from the Greek cities of the Aegean coast, including Herodotos' own Halikarnassos, and to proclaim a new naval alliance to deter Persian resurgence in the region. Herodotos will have witnessed as a child the 'liberation' of Halikarnassos from the Persians and its transference to Athenian rule.

The Persian Wars were truly a turning point in world history. They barred the way to the further westward expansion of the Persian Empire and allowed the fledgling Athenian democracy, which had been founded just a decade or two earlier (508/7 BC), to exert its influence throughout the Aegean. The victory also changed the way the Greeks thought about themselves. It confirmed their belief in the native superiority of Greeks over non-Greeks and of Greek political institutions over Persian absolut-

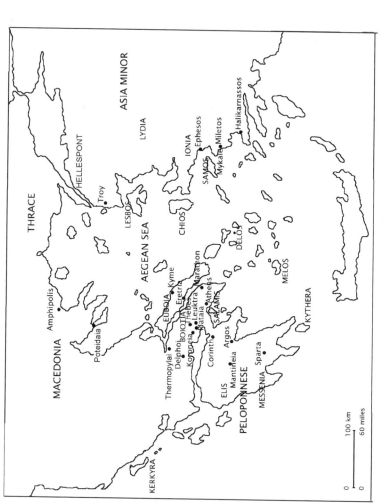

Fig. 2 Greece and the Aegean in the fifth and fourth centuries BC

ism, and added a derogatory tone to the Greek term for all such outsiders: *barbaroi* or 'barbarians', a word coined initially to represent the unintelligible sound of non-Greek speech. Less than ten years afterwards, the tragedian Aischylos put on a play in Athens called *The Persians*, in which the victory was celebrated as a triumph of Greek, and especially Athenian, valour against eastern despotism (472 BC). It is understandable, then, that Herodotos too should have wanted to commemorate and explain the Greek success and that in doing so he should be drawn to that other tale of Greek conflict with the east, Homer's *Iliad*. More surprising, perhaps, is that Herodotos should share with Homer an understanding of and sympathy for the non-Greek cultures which he describes, a feature which was later in antiquity to be seen as something of an embarrassment.

Herodotos was later dubbed the 'father of history' (Cicero, *Laws* 1.5), but even in the opening lines of his work, he announces his own debt to Homer:

> Herodotos of Halikarnassos here puts on display his research (*historie*). His purpose is that the things that have been done by men should not be forgotten with the passage of time, and that the great and amazing deeds put on display by both Greeks and barbarians should not be deprived of glory – in particular the reason why they went to war against each other. (1.1)

Herodotos' theme, like Homer's, is a war between east and west, between Greeks and non-Greeks. He sets out to explain the causes of the conflict, 'the reason why they went to war against each other'. This line is reminiscent of the opening of the *Iliad* and makes clear that Herodotos saw himself as writing within the Homeric tradition. Indeed he goes on to trace – fancifully – the origins of the Persian Wars back to the Trojan War, though later he will claim that the war he is describing was greater than any war in history – a claim obviously made with a sideways glance at Homer (7.20). It is noticeable, furthermore, that Herodotos' declared purpose in writing about the war is commemorative, that is, that those who fought receive their proper 'glory' – another Homeric concept, recalling the description of Achilles singing of the 'glorious deeds of men' (*Iliad* 9.189).

kleos

Herodotos and the new rationalism

But if Herodotos was inspired by and tried to rival Homer, there were other influences on him too. In the opening line he declares that his work is *historie* – the Ionic dialect form for the more usual Greek *historia* – from which the modern word 'history' is derived. This is the first recorded instance of the use of the word. It was later to develop the meaning which has come down to us, a narrative of past events, though with emphasis on the political and the military; but in the fifth century BC it referred rather to the process than the result, something along the lines of 'research' or 'enquiry'. In this spirit of enquiry Herodotos was almost certainly influenced by another intellectual movement which had been taking place in the generations before him in the Ionian Greek cities north of Halikarnassos. Thinkers such as Thales and Anaximander of Miletos, or Herakleitos of Ephesos, men whom we know by the collective title of 'Pre-Socratic Philosophers', had begun the process of enquiry into the natural world. Their works survive for us only in rather enigmatic fragments, but the questions which they asked were in the order of 'What is the world made of?' 'What gives nature continuity when all is in flux?' 'How are eclipses to be explained?' The answer given to this latter question notably did not involve appeal to divine intervention; the world was to be explained on purely rational grounds. Shortly before Herodotos wrote his work, a writer called Hekataios, another native of Miletos, composed a work entitled *Journey Around the Earth*, in which he recorded information both cultural and geographical which he had gleaned in his travels or reading. He famously began another of his works, the *Genealogies*, with the words: 'Hekataios of Miletos speaks thus. I write what seems to me to be true; for the Greeks have many tales which, it seems to me, are absurd' (frag. 1). Herodotos himself slyly corrects Hekataios on a number of points (e.g. 2.20-3), but Hekataios' own rationalising spirit of critical enquiry, written up in prose and in the same Ionic Greek dialect, must have influenced Herodotos. Indeed, Herodotos even seems at one point to quote him, when he talks of 'the ill-considered tales of the Greeks' (2.45).

Herodotos proclaims, then, at the start of his work that his narrative is based on the fruits of 'research'. This emphasis on research, in which he probably includes travel, questioning of eye-witnesses and collation of oral tradition, and the consequent acknowledgment that the truth may be hard to discover, is both a new departure and a tremendously significant moment in the development of the practice of history. Neither in Homer, nor in the narratives of the Hebrew Bible, some of which were being written at roughly the same time, is any acknowledgment given to the problems of sources and bias. But after Herodotos it would be considered an essential part of the historian's task to distinguish truth from untruth, good sources from bad. Herodotos himself makes many references to his sources of information, often the oral traditions of the peoples whom he claims to have encountered on his travels, and refers often enough to the difficulty of deciding on the correct account. This new critical attitude to the truth becomes immediately apparent. After declaring his purpose to find out the causes of the conflict between Greeks and Persians, Herodotos begins with a series of events set in the distant past. The Phoenicians kidnapped a woman from Argos called Io, a figure well-known in mythology. This sets in train a further set of mutual kidnappings of women on both sides, leading ultimately to Paris' kidnapping of Helen and the Greek expedition against Troy to get her back. So far, so Homeric. But Herodotos' rationalising spirit soon becomes clear. The Io of myth was loved by Zeus and consequently turned into a heifer by Zeus' jealous wife. But for Herodotos Io is merely the victim of abduction by pirates. Similarly Europe, another of Zeus' erotic conquests, is according to Herodotos carried across the sea not, as tradition had it, by Zeus in the form of a bull, but by Greek sailors in retaliation for the abduction of Io. But Herodotos does not limit himself merely to rationalising the myths. He also records, in a spirit of cultural even-handedness which is everywhere apparent in his work, not only the Greek versions of these myths but also some versions current among the Persians and Phoenicians. The Persians made out that the Greeks blew the rape of Helen out of all proportion: women get raped, they argue, but it is foolish to start a war over such a minor matter. The Phoenician version is even more radical: Io was not kidnapped or raped by their ship's captain, but rather *eloped* with him after getting pregnant. Herodotos concludes:

> This is what the Persians and Phoenicians say. For my part I will not declare that this or that story is true, but I will name the man whom I myself know to have wronged the Greeks, and so go forward with my history in this way, detailing both small and great cities of men alike. For many cities that were once great have become small, and those that were great in my time were small formerly. Knowing therefore that human prosperity never remains the same, I will make mention of both alike. (1.5)

Various things are worth noting here. First, Herodotos declares himself uncertain about the truth of the stories of kidnapping and counter-kidnapping. A critical spirit is apparent, and a critical attitude to sources. Elsewhere he declares that he considers it his duty to *report* what he has heard (literally, 'to say what is being said'), but not bound to *believe* it (7.152). Secondly, Herodotos makes a clear distinction between the distant past, where the truth is hard to discover, and recent history. Such recent history can be investigated with more certainty, and this is where Herodotos will concentrate his effort. He makes a deft glance towards the opening of Homer's *Odyssey* and an implicit comparison of himself to Odysseus, who 'saw the cities of many men' (*Odyssey* 1.3), but at the same time he abandons the Homeric time-frame and moves to the man 'whom *I myself know* to have done unprovoked wrong to the Greeks': Croesus, king of Lydia until 546 BC, that is, until roughly a century before Herodotos was writing. The rejection of the distant and mythological past and the concentration on the recent past, that is, on periods for which eye-witnesses and oral tradition and possibly written records remained, would be a feature common to most later historians. The third notable aspect of this passage is that Herodotos displays a concern to place responsibility and blame, a desire to commemorate. In the opening lines of his work he had declared his intention 'that the things that have been done by men should not be forgotten with the passage of time, and that the great and amazing deeds put on display by both Greeks and barbarians should not be deprived of glory' (1.1). It is this same concern for commemoration, and the highly moral sensibility which accompanies it, which will lead to a concern for recording the names of those who distinguished themselves either for courage and loyalty or for cowardice, treachery or cruelty. This concern for commemoration will also lead him to catalogue the 'amazing' wonders, whether natural or man-made, of the countries which he discusses. He describes Egypt at length, 'because' he declares, 'in no other land are there so many marvellous things' (2.35) – such as, for example, the crocodile (2.68-70). Similarly, when discussing events on the island of Samos he describes what he declares to be 'the three greatest works of all the Greeks', including a water-tunnel said to be seven stades, or almost a mile, long (3.60).

Finally, there is a strong philosophical tone to this passage. Human prosperity never remains the same. Cities rise and cities fall. This is a thought which is persistent throughout Herodotos' work. It plainly owes something to the intellectual climate of the Ionian cities, where men like Herakleitos were arguing from the physical world that 'everything is in flux', that nothing stays the same – as Herakleitos was later famously reported as saying, 'you cannot step into the same river twice' (frag. 12 D-K). But the thought is also a moral one. Human prosperity changes; the great fall and the small become great. A persistent strand of Herodotos' work emphasises this fact. The great should not become arrogant, or they too will be brought low. Fortune is a wheel, which never stops turning, as Croesus himself comes to see after his own humiliation (1.207). The story of the Persian Wars is, as we shall see, presented as an illustration of this profoundly moral, and rather fatalistic, view of life.

The mirror of Herodotos

Herodotos' work is traditionally divided into nine books, which together run to about 600 pages in modern editions – traditionally, because such book-divisions probably represent little more than the amount that could be held on a single papyrus scroll. But it is only from Book 5, where Herodotos narrates the opening moves of the Ionian revolt (499-494 BC), that the Persian Wars proper begin. Books 5 and 6 narrate the failure of the revolt, caused in large part by disunity among the rebel Greek cities, and the David-and-Goliath victory of the Athenians at Marathon in 490 BC. Books 7-9 follow the invasion of 480-479 BC, as much from the Persian viewpoint as from the Greek, and conclude with the Greeks crossing the Aegean and expelling Persian garrisons from the coastal cities of Thrace and Asia Minor.

The first half of the work (Books 1-4) gives the background to the conflict, tracing the rise of the Persian Empire from a small nomadic people, through their conquest first of Lydia and its king, Croesus, from whom they inherited hegemony over the Ionian Greeks, and then of Egypt, and finally their abortive invasion of Scythia. These first books are more episodic than the later ones, and transport the reader to strange distant lands, redolent of oriental wealth and intrigue. We read of King Kandaules of Lydia boasting of his wife's beauty and forcing Gyges, one of his palace guards, to hide behind the door of her boudoir and watch her as she undresses. But the queen catches sight of Gyges in the shadows, and declares to him later that he must either kill the king who shamed her, or die himself (1.8-13). We find ourselves with Arion the lyre player who is cast overboard by a treacherous ship's crew, but is rescued by a dolphin and turns up at Corinth to accuse his smug betrayers (1.23-4). We learn of the strange customs of the Egyptians, a people whom Herodotos admits were far more ancient than the Greeks and to whom he devotes a whole book (Book 2). In Egypt, Herodotos would have his readers believe, all is topsy-turvy: the women stand to urinate and the men sit down; girls work as prostitutes to earn their dowries; and dogs and cats are held sacred.

It would be tempting to label these stories, and the first half of Herodotos' work as a whole, as mere story-telling, or travel-writing, digressions from the main theme of Herodotos' work, the Persian Wars themselves. Some have gone further, even in antiquity, and accused him of being gullible and garrulous. This would be a great injustice. For one thing, we must remember that Herodotos' view of what *historia* meant was far different from our own. Geography and ethnography, the exploration of the lands and cultures of other people, were to remain for the ancients an important component of history. But in fact the descriptions of alien cultures serve a profound end within Herodotos' work as a whole. If the Greeks could beat the Persians, though overwhelmingly outnumbered, what made them so special? By describing the cultures of alien peoples, Persians, Scythians, Egyptians, Herodotos holds up, as it were, a mirror to his own Greek culture. That is, by describing cultures so different to the Greeks, Herodotos gives to his readers a reverse image of what they themselves are, a standard against which to measure themselves. The Persians, once they have achieved their conquests, are luxury-loving and all, even the greatest of them, are slaves to a single master. The Greeks by contrast are, in Herodotos' ideal projection, frugal, the hard products of a hard, unforgiving land; they serve no master but law itself.

This contrast between Greek love of freedom and Persian autocracy is one which recurs throughout Herodotos' work. The clearest example is in the so-called Constitutional Debate in Book 3. The scene is set in the Persian Court at Sousa in 521 BC, some twenty years before the Ionian revolt. A conspiracy of seven Persian noblemen has assassinated a usurper of the Persian throne. They meet to decide what form of government should be adopted. Three of the conspirators speak, each recommending the establishment of an alternative form of government: democracy, oligarchy (that is, the rule of a few aristocrats), and monarchy. A vote is taken and monarchy wins out (3.80-4).

The most interesting thing about the Constitutional Debate is that the incident which it describes could not possibly have taken place. Democracy was not established even in Athens until over a decade later than this incident is said to have taken place, and it is almost unthinkable that Persian noblemen even contemplated setting up such a system. Most probably Herodotos has invented the speeches in order to explore an issue – freedom versus autocracy – which was so central to his construction of what it meant to be Greek. Indeed, the invention of speeches, a literary feature inherited from Homer, was to be a constant feature in the work of ancient historians. Such invention allowed the writer to explore deeper issues of morality and motivation, and to expose the workings of the minds of his protagonists. Thus Herodotos uses his fictional Constitutional Debate to characterise both the Persians, as wedded to monarchy, and, by implication, the Greeks, as enlightened and free.

Perhaps Herodotos' interest in the clash of cultures, and his tendency to invent speeches to explore deeper issues, is best exemplified in the conversation he dramatises in Book 7 between Xerxes and the exiled Spartan king Demaratos, who has sought refuge at the Persian court and accompanies the invasion force. Xerxes asks him who the Spartans are and how such a small city can think to stand up to the might of Persia. Demaratos replies:

'Your majesty, you order me to speak nothing but the truth and to say nothing that you will find out to be false. Greece has always had poverty as its companion, but it has acquired virtue, the product of wisdom and strong law. By using virtue, Greece defends herself from poverty and tyranny. Now I praise all Greeks that live in those Dorian lands; yet I do not intend at the present time to speak about all, but only about the Spartans. First, they will never accept from you conditions that bring slavery on Greece; secondly, they will meet you in battle even if all the rest of the Greeks are on your side. But as to their number, do not ask how many there are who are able to do this. Whether they happen to have a thousand men in the field, or less or more than this, these men will fight you.'   (7.102)

Xerxes laughs when he hears this. How could a small number possibly think of standing up to a huge army especially, he reasons, if they are free?

'For if were they ruled by one man', Xerxes said, 'as is our custom, they might out of fear of him show greater courage than is natural, and by being compelled by the whip they might go to fight with small numbers against many. But if they were allowed to go free they would not do either of these things.'   (7.103)

These words which Herodotos puts into Xerxes' mouth (for Herodotos could surely have no way of knowing the exact details of the conversation) characterise both him and the Greeks. Xerxes is despotic and arrogant, unable to contemplate the possibility of courage or self-sacrifice, or of his own defeat. The Greeks, by implication, are characterised as brave and freedom-loving, serving not out of fear of an autocrat but in defence of their own states and liberty. As Demaratos concludes 'Although they are free, they are not wholly free; for they have a master over them, Law, whom they fear much more than your men fear you' (7.104).

Herodotos the tragedian: hybris *and* nemesis

The proud are humbled; the poor become great. Xerxes' arrogance and megalomaniac over-confidence find their outworking in his humiliation by the alliance of tiny Greek states which defeat him. This brings us to a final and, for us, striking feature of Herodotos' work, one which was inherited again from Homer and was to be imitated by later historians: its profoundly moral sense. Central to Herodotos' presentation of the Persian Wars is the belief that pride comes before a fall, that too much success is dangerous, and that overconfidence leads to humiliation, or – to put it in more specifically religious terms, as Herodotos often does – when men forget that they are mere men, when they lord it over others and challenge the gods, divine vengeance will not be long in coming. The Greek words for this set of ideas are *hybris*, which means any kind of insulting, dishonouring behaviour, including that directed towards the gods, and *nemesis* (divine revenge), which can be seen as a natural counterpart of *hybris*.

The story of Xerxes and the Persian invasions of Greece, then, is an example writ large of this natural law, that *hybris* is followed by *nemesis* in an inevitable cycle. Xerxes' megalomania is made very clear at the start of Book 7 where he declares to a council of Persian noblemen his plan to invade Greece:

'If we subdue these men [the Athenians], and their neighbours who live in the land of Pelops the Phrygian [the Peloponnesians], we shall make the borders of Persian territory reach God's heaven; for the sun will behold no land that borders ours, for I will make all one country together, when I have passed through the whole of Europe.'

(7.8)

Xerxes' uncle Artabanos advises caution, warning him, ominously, that 'God allows pride in no-one but himself' (7.10). But Xerxes rejects his advice, thus confirming his folly and leading the reader to expect disaster to follow. Surprisingly, Xerxes decides later to change his mind and to cancel the invasion, but he is prevented from doing so by a recurring dream which urges him to follow through his plans: the model for this is surely the dream which Zeus sends to Agamemnon in the *Iliad* (2.1-47). This certainly suggests the working of the divine will. But Xerxes' own pride and megalomania are never in doubt. He beats the Hellespont with whips when a storm breaks down a pontoon bridge (7.35); later it is the sea and its squalls which will repeatedly destroy his fleet. He frequently boasts of the strength of his army, and laughs at Greek attempts to resist, ignoring miracles and omens which predict disaster (e.g. 8.35-9, 65). Finally, against all his expectations he watches his mighty fleet crushed in the narrow straits of Salamis. The man who was not content to rule Asia, and thought to add Europe to his domain, is humbled and brought low.

If Xerxes' invasion of Greece in Books 7-9 can be seen as the supreme example of *hybris* leading to *nemesis*, there are various other examples, narrated on a smaller scale, which prepare the reader for it. Indeed these repeated cycles of pride and humiliation impose some unity on the diverse material which fills Herodotos' early books. The story of Croesus of Lydia, whose rise and fall are narrated in Book 1, can be read in this way. We learn from the first that Croesus is doomed. His ancestor Gyges came to the throne, as we have seen (p. 19), by murdering the legitimate king. In consequence of this treachery, a Delphic oracle forecasts divine vengeance on his family in the fifth generation (1.13). But as in the case of Xerxes and his dream, divine predestination does not preclude human responsibility. Croesus' arrogance is brought out most clearly in his conversation with the Athenian law-giver Solon, a man famed for his wisdom. Croesus shows Solon all his treasures and then asks him if he had ever seen a more fortunate man. He is amazed by the answer: Solon names several ordinary Greeks, and concludes with words which are prophetic of Croesus' fall: 'We must look to the end of every matter, and see how it will turn out. For there are many to whom god has shown blessedness and then has ruined utterly' (1.32). Croesus rejects Solon's words, just as Xerxes will reject the wise advice of Artabanos. Herodotos concludes 'But after Solon's departure, great *nemesis* from God seized Croesus: as I guess because he supposed himself to be more blessed than any other man' (1.34). This divine revenge comes upon Croesus in two ways. First his son is killed, despite all Croesus' efforts to protect him. Secondly, over-confidence leads him to attack the growing Persian Empire, and to lose both his throne and his wealth. As he stands on the pyre about to be burnt at the stake, Croesus admits the wisdom of Solon's words (1.86).

This conception of the world, in which *hybris* brings *nemesis* and in which the gods' will prevails, has certain similarities with the conception of the world found in many of the tragedies which were being put on the stage in Athens in Herodotos' time and shortly after. In Sophokles' play, *Oedipus Tyrannus*, the main character Oedipus inherits a curse from his ancestors and is told that he is destined to commit the outrageous crimes of killing his father and sleeping with his mother. In trying to avoid this fate, Oedipus unwittingly brings it on himself, as the audience looks on helplessly. In the *Oedipus Tyrannus*, then, we see an intelligent man who has reached the heights of power by his own efforts, but who falls both because of his own *hybris* and, more disturbingly, because the gods had willed it so. But even more relevant to Herodotos is Aischylos' tragedy, *The Persians*, performed half a century earlier in 472 BC. The play is set at the Persian court, as news arrives of the defeat at Salamis. Here the link is explicitly made between Xerxes' overconfidence and his humiliation at the hands of a jealous divinity. It is just possible that as a child Herodotos could have seen this play being performed, and he may well have been influenced by it. But it is probably more helpful to think not so much of the direct influence of the genre of tragedy on Herodotos' work, but rather that both Herodotos' *Histories* and the contemporary tragedies of Aischylos and Sophokles reflect a common way of looking at and interpreting the world. Both share a tendency to see causation as acting independently on both a human and a divine level. Thus for Herodotos Xerxes is indeed led by the gods through a dream to invade Greece, and his humiliation is indeed seen as the last in a long series in which the cycle of *hybris* and *nemesis* is played out. But his decision to invade and his defeat are also explained, at much greater length, on a human and political level. He wishes to punish Athens and Eretria, and to add to his Empire. We are also told of the personal motives which Mardonios, his cousin, and Hippias, the exiled tyrant of Athens, had for encouraging the invasion (7.5-6). So human and divine causation exist side by side. Similarly, if Xerxes' huge forces can be seen as a symbol of his *hybris*, as seems to be suggested in Artabanos' speech (7.10) and elsewhere, Herodotos also brings out the immense problems that such great numbers of men and ships caused him at the military and logistical level, as indeed Artabanos predicted (7.49): his fleet falls prey to storms and shipwreck, and is unable to fight properly in the enclosed waters of Salamis.

We may be surprised at the religious and moral element in Herodotos. To us it might appear to sit rather uncomfortably with the 'rational' elements in his work: his emphasis on research, his analysis of sources, his tendency to rationalise the mythical and the incredible, his interest in causation on the human level. But that would be to import our own notions of what history should be. Indeed, modern historians are beginning to realise that constructing a narrative, selecting and prioritising, always involves some kind of interpretation. Consciously or not, all historians impose some sort of story or meaning on to the mass of data which they have at their disposal. Herodotos, and all the Greek and Roman historians who came after him, understood this well and looked to history for more than just a narration of events. They expected the historian, through his narrative, to teach or to explore wider issues, be they religious, political or moral.

Chapter 3

Thucydides

Thucydides and the Peloponnesian War

The Persians were expelled from the Aegean by 478 BC, but by the time Herodotos was finishing his work in perhaps the late 430s, the united front put up by Athens and Sparta against the common enemy must have seemed a distant memory. The power-vacuum left in the wake of Persia's defeat was immediately filled by Athens, the new imperial power. She lost no time in setting up a naval league, which included most of the coastal and island states of the Aegean, many of them recently liberated from Persia. As fear of Persian resurgence faded, so Athens began increasingly to treat these supposed 'allies' as her own subjects, and to regard the Delian League as her own Empire. Meanwhile, although Sparta was busy with her own parochial concerns in the Peloponnese, she could not fail to be anxious at Athens' growing power. At the end of the 460s, Athens was fighting a desultory war with one of Sparta's most important allies, Corinth. A thirty-year peace treaty was signed between Athens and Sparta, more in hope than expectation, in 446. But by the 430s the stage was set for a major confrontation between the two powers. A protracted period of conflict, presented by Thucydides as a single war and so regarded by modern historians, who give it the name the 'Peloponnesian War', began in 431 and lasted down to 404 BC when Athens surrendered, her walls were pulled down and her empire dissolved.

Thucydides, an Athenian aristocrat, witnessed the war at first hand. He was probably in his late twenties when it broke out, and in 424 he was elected one of the ten Athenian commanders for that year. He himself describes how he was posted to the region of Thrace on the northern shores of the Aegean, where his family had estates, but failed to save the city of Amphipolis from Spartan attack (Thuc. 4.104-7). For this failure, whether deservedly or not, he was condemned to exile by the Athenian democracy. He claims, in a passage written after his banishment (5.26), that being in exile gave him access to both sides of the conflict. This passage is particularly interesting, as we shall see, because in it Thucydides defends his decision to classify all the events of 431-404 within the scope of a single 'Peloponnesian War' (see below, p. 30). An uneasy truce was made after ten years of war in 421 (the Peace of Nikias), and it seems that at first Thucydides, like many others, considered that this point marked the end of the war. He is at pains to point out, however, that the truce, which was broken officially only in 413, was a phony one, and that the conflict lasted in reality, unbroken, from 431 to 404. For all that, however, Thucydides' account breaks off with the war in full flow in 411, probably as a result of his own death shortly after the end of the war.

Thucydides' methodology

In choosing to write about a war, Thucydides was obviously setting himself in the same tradition as Homer and Herodotos – and plainly inviting comparison with them. Indeed he seems to have been acutely aware of the problem of comparison with his predecessors. This is particularly clear in the opening words of his history. They not only recall the prologues of Homer and Herodotos, but also attempt to set Thucydides' own work apart from them:

> Thucydides of Athens wrote the account of the war *which the Peloponnesians and Athens waged against each other* (cf. *Iliad* 1.8; Herodotos 1.1), having begun as soon as it started in the expectation that it would be a great war and more worthy of record than those in the past, judging from the fact that both sides went into it at the peak of readiness and seeing that the rest of the Greek world was lining up with one side or the other, some at once, others intending to do so. For this was the greatest upheaval to affect the Greeks and a considerable number of barbarians – one might even say, a very large part of mankind. For while it was impossible to get clear information about the preceding period and the events even before that, on account of the passage of time, nevertheless, on the basis of the evidence which I can trust from such a distant view, I believe that the earlier periods were not great in wars or in anything else.   (1.1.1-2)

His war, Thucydides maintains, was greater and more destructive than any previous conflict. The first chapters of Book 1, conventionally known as the *Archaeology* ('the section on the distant past') consist of a detailed defence of this point, arguing that the importance and scale of the Trojan War have been exaggerated by Homer and that, although the Persian Wars were greater than all previous conflicts, they were decided by merely 'two battles by land and two by sea' (1.23) – in contrast to the much more drawn-out Peloponnesian War.

But it is not just in the scale of their respective wars that Thucydides claims to be superior to his predecessors, but in his methods:

> Now the early period I have found to be something like I have described, although it is difficult to believe any and every piece of testimony. For men accept from each other's hearsay reports about events in the past, even when they concern their own countries, with a uniform lack of examination.
>
> (1.20.1)

Thucydides goes on to cite some examples taken from Herodotos, whom he does not name, which are meant to prove the latter's lax methods of examining and sifting evidence. Poets, he concludes, exaggerate and 'story-tellers' (Herodotos is obviously in his sights here) 'aim at being entertaining to listen to rather than truthful'.

There is plainly here a certain amount of literary rivalry and one-up-manship. But this emphasis on the importance of sifting evidence, and of the potential conflict between the attractions of entertainment, of telling a good story, and the rigours of truthful reporting, albeit in the context of rivalry with a literary competitor, is one of Thucydides' most significant contributions to the development of historical method. He goes on to set out his own practice in one of the most well-known and notoriously difficult passages in ancient literature:

> As for the speeches that were made by the different parties, either before the war or when they were involved in it, it has been difficult both for me – in the case of the speeches I heard myself – and for those who informed me about speeches made elsewhere, to remember precisely what was said. But I have put things in accordance with what I thought each speaker would have said given what was required in the situation, keeping as close as possible to the general gist of what was actually said.
>
> As for the actions that were carried out in the war, I did not think it right to describe them on the basis of what I learnt from chance informants or in accordance with what I thought, but to investigate each point with as much precision as possible, in the case both of events at which I was present and of those which I heard from others. Finding out what happened involved great effort because those who were present at the various specific actions did not give consistent

reports, but they varied according to their support of one side or the other, or according to their memory.   (1.22.1-3)

Thucydides seems here to divide the events of the war into two categories, speech (*logos*) and action (*ergon*): a common ancient division, in which speech – debates in the Assembly, negotiations – are seen as events just as much as battles or other military actions (on Thucydides' speeches, see below, pp. 33-6). In both Homer and Herodotos narrative had been punctuated with direct speech, as it is in Thucydides. But for both these types of event, Thucydides lays claim to special standards of accuracy. These claims are based on two principles, both of extreme importance for later historians. The first is that he will limit himself to events either at which he was present himself or for which he was able to find eye-witnesses. Herodotos had been happy to report hearsay about the distant past; but for Thucydides, and for most subsequent historians, original history would deal only with contemporary events or with the very recent past, events for which eye-witnesses were still available. Secondly, Thucydides notes the tendency of eye-witnesses to contradict each other, whether through hazy recollection or through downright bias. Eye-witness reports must be sifted and set against each other, with particular attention given to the possibilities of bias. These principles may not of themselves have been revolutionary. Herodotos himself was aware of the problems of conflicting sources (e.g. 7.152), and was in fact a good deal more forth-coming than Thucydides in citing who his sources were and on what points they differed. But what is significant is that Thucydides for the first time gives explicit expression not only to the problem of sources, but also to a methodology of analysing and judging their reliability.

The causes of the Peloponnesian War

Thucydides' skill in sifting evidence is seen most clearly in his analysis of the causes of the Peloponnesian War, which takes up most of the rest of Book 1. This section is remarkable for the distinctions it makes both between the immediate catalysts of the war and the real underlying cause, and between what was alleged by both sides (their propaganda), and what really motivated them. After emphasising once again the scale of suffering brought about by this war, he continues:

The war began when the Athenians and Peloponnesians broke the thirty years' truce, which they had made after the capture of Euboia [446 BC]. As to why they broke the truce, I have first set down the grounds and disputes, so that no one may ever have to inquire for the reasons why so great a war broke out among the Greeks. I believe that the *truest explanation* (*prophasis*), although it has been least often expressed, was the growth of Athenian power, which frightened the Spartans and forced them into war. But the *reasons* (*aitiai*) *publicly alleged* on both sides which led them to break the truce and declare war were as follows ...   (1.23.4-6)

The real reason for the Spartan declaration of war, then, was their fear of Athens, not the events that actually precipitated the war. But Thucydides now proceeds to recount in great detail two of these incidents which sparked off the war. Both involved Athens' intervention in the affairs of two colonies of Corinth.

In 432 BC Athens concluded an alliance with Kerkyra (Corfu), thus indirectly taking the side of a colony against its mother-city. She also laid siege to Poteidaia in northern Greece. Poteidaia was a member of the Athenian empire, but also a colony of Corinth, and Athens' action was seen in Corinth as a provocation. The Corinthians appealed to Sparta, who reluctantly declared war. In order to explore the motives and pressures which resulted in the two sides being pulled into war, Thucydides reconstructs the arguments which might have taken place in the decisive meetings of the Athenian Assembly and the Peloponnesian League. Finally, after carefully dating the outbreak of war ('in the fourteenth year of the thirty years' truce, which was made after the Euboian war'), he concludes by restating his theory as to its underlying cause:

The Spartans voted that the treaty had been broken and that they must go to war, not so much because they were persuaded by the speeches of their allies as because they feared that the Athenians might otherwise become more powerful, seeing as they did that the majority of Greece was already subject to them.   (1.88)

To prove this thesis – that it was growth of Athenian power and the fear which it caused in Sparta which led her to declare war – Thucydides now goes back in time to review the roughly fifty years between the end of the Persian Wars and the outbreak of the Peloponnesian War (478-432 BC). Conventionally known as the *pentekontaetia* or 'fifty-year period', this section (1.89-118) is our only early narrative source for this important epoch and, not fortuitously, begins at the point where Herodotos broke off. Although some scholars have considered the *pentekontaetia* biased in favour of either Athens or Sparta, Thucydides' analysis, that the causes of the war should not be seen in the immediate flash-points but in the underlying factors, has never really been superseded and stands as an early, and impressive, example of the theorisation of inter-state conflict. It is no surprise to find that Thucydides' language here has marked similarities with the language of contemporary medical writers, themselves interested in causation, though of a rather different kind. Thucydides concludes the narrative of the 'fifty years' with these words:

It was in this period that the Athenians established their empire more securely and advanced their own power greatly. Although the Spartans were aware of what was happening, they made no attempt to intervene, except to a small extent, and remained inactive most of the time, since they had never been quick to go to war except when forced, and at that time were somewhat hampered by wars of their own. But finally the power of the Athenians began to emerge clearly and they began to interfere with Sparta's alliances. At that point the Spartans could bear it no longer and began to think that they must attack with all their energy and destroy the power of Athens, if they could, by undertaking this war.   (1.118.2)

With these words Thucydides' begins the history of the Peloponnesian War proper. The first half of his work (until 5.25) deals with the first ten years of the war ('the Archidamian War'), down to the Peace of Nikias in 421 BC, which Thucydides seems to have initially conceived as the end of the war (see above, pp. 25-6). In 5.26, however, which forms a kind of second prologue, and which must have been written after the surrender of Athens in 404 BC, Thucydides asserts the belief, as we have seen, that the war should be regarded as a single whole stretching from 431-404:

The same Thucydides, an Athenian, has recorded these events too [i.e. those after 421 BC] in the order in which they occurred, by summers and winters, up to the time when the Spartans and their allies put an end to the empire of the Athenians and took the Long Walls and Peiraieus. Up to that event the war lasted twenty-seven years in all; and if anyone does not think it right to consider the intervening truce as part of the war, his claim will not be correct ...
                                        (5.26.1-2)

Thus begins the second section of Thucydides' work, which consists of the narrative of the phoney peace of 421-413 BC, probably unfinished (5.26-116), a section on the disastrous Sicilian Expedition of 415-413 BC

[Books 6-7], and then in Book 8 the early events of the second phase of the war. This final book, which is unfinished, breaks off abruptly in the course of the events of 411 BC.

Thucydides and 'scientific' history

Thucydides' contribution to the development of the genre and practice of history was immense. First of all, he implicitly defined what history meant: his conception of the scope of history as being essentially limited to events on the grand stage of politics or war, and limited to the very recent past, was one followed by most ancient historians after him. Gone are the anecdotes, the interest in personalities, and – with a few exceptions – the discussions of foreign lands and customs which we find in Herodotos. Gone also is any reference to the gods or to divine intervention. Rather, in Thucydides we find an obsession with war and politics, and a concern to demonstrate causation on purely rational grounds. Furthermore, Thucydides' awareness of the importance of chronology and his attempts to date the events he described 'by summers and winters' from the outbreak of the war, were revolutionary, and rarely matched in the ancient world. Finally, his emphasis on the importance of checking eye-witness testimony, and on the possibilities of bias in informants, set standards which are still of great relevance today.

These striking features of Thucydides' declared methodology have earned for him a reputation amongst some modern scholars as a 'scientific historian' – that is, as one who applied the methodologies of modern science to his evaluation of evidence. His account of the years before and during the Peloponnesian War have accordingly gained amongst some an almost scriptural status. Moreover, this admiration for Thucydides' work has almost certainly been increased by an appreciation of his prose style. Whereas Herodotos' Greek is flowing and easy, Thucydides' is difficult, dense, full of circumstantial detail, and requires careful attention from the reader. This difficult style, combined with the almost total lack of references to sources of information or of statements of doubt on Thucydides' own part, has created an impression of credibility, objectivity and seriousness – of, as one scholar has put it, 'magisterial authority'.

In part this reputation for objectivity is deserved. At very few points have inaccuracies of fact been discovered in his account. But we should be careful not to idealise Thucydides. Thucydides' account is certainly not fully objective nor does it include everything we would like to know. For example, after the section on early history, the *Archaeology*, he says next to nothing about economic factors, a theme which would be considered essential to any modern study of the Peloponnesian, or any other, war. We know from an inscription (ML 69 = *IG* 1³ 71) that in 425 BC the Athenians almost doubled the tribute that they demanded from the member states of their empire. This change is extremely significant, both in terms of what it shows about Athenian imperialism, but also for the light it sheds on the Peloponnesian War, Thucydides' main theme. Modern historians see in this event an indication of the costliness of the war for Athens and an explanation of the willingness of many of the elites in the allied states to revolt as the war dragged on. But Thucydides says nothing of it. Nor does he give any figures for the income or expenditure of the two sides, or where, and with what difficulty, raw materials such as timber for ship-building were obtained.

So Thucydides does not tell us all we would like to know. Nor, in fact, does he seem always to have been totally objective – a fact which perhaps should surprise less than it has. An aristocrat himself, and one who suffered at the hands of the popular Assembly when he was exiled from Athens for his failure to save Amphipolis, it was perhaps natural that he would idealise the aristocratic leader Perikles, who died two years after the war began. This idealisation of Perikles is clearest in an important passage which Thucydides seems to have inserted into Book 2 towards the end of the war (2.65). Writing with the benefit of hindsight, from a vantage-point towards the end of the war, he here provides for the reader a look forward at Athens' fortunes after Perikles' death. He declares that under Perikles 'what was in name a democracy was in reality the rule of the first citizen' (2.65.9) – a statement which betrays markedly anti-democratic leanings and seems little backed up by other evidence. (Indeed, for all Thucydides' claims, Perikles is very little mentioned by writers of the next generations.) This admiration for Perikles, furthermore, leads Thucydides here to pour scorn on Perikles' less than aristocratic successors, men like Kleon or Theramenes, and to lament that Perikles' defensive wait-and-see strategy for the war was abandoned. But many modern historians doubt whether this defensive policy, even without the loss of the fleet in Sicily, could ever have worked: Perikles failed to take into account the threat posed by Persia, which ultimately saw its own interests as best served in backing Sparta and in lending her the financial assistance required to wear Athens down. As it turned out, the more aggressive policy of men like Kleon, whom Thucydides so disparaged, may well have offered Athens her only real hope of victory. Indeed, in this same retrospective passage, Thucydides does seem to accept that the invasion of Sicily was not as foolish as he had presented later on in the work; it failed, he says, through foolish decisions at home, by which he probably means in particular through the recall and subsequent exile of the aristocratic Alkibiades, its prime instigator and one of its three generals (2.65.11-12). By the time he wrote this, Thucydides had probably witnessed not only Alkibiades' brilliance later in the war but also the massive effect of Persian financial subsidy of the Spartan fleet. Perikles' defensive policy may no longer have seemed so attractive to him as it did some years earlier. We should not be surprised by these omissions, oversights or biases. Every historian must make choices about what is to be included and what excluded, and these choices are determined by his or her own values and those of his or her society, as well as by his or her personal biases and interests. This means that truly 'scientific' history, is never possible: history is not a science, if by that we mean that it can attain an objective and unitary truth, a truth which can be verified by objective methods. Rather, history is always, to some extent, the creation of the historian, who selects, who gives his or her own emphases to the material that is included, and who presents such material in a way that makes sense to and interests his or her own intended readers. Indeed, although Thucydides' attention to detail is striking, it is as much in the interpretation and order which he has imposed on his material that we should see his greatness.

Thucydides the artist

Thucydides' own hand is most apparent in the speeches. They take up a large part of Thucydides' history, as they had done in Herodotos and as they do in most ancient historians. Indeed, as we have seen, the practice of inserting speeches into the narrative goes back to Homer. This emphasis on set speeches is also a reflection of the intrinsically oral nature of politics and society in ancient Greece, and of the particular interest in oratory and its techniques which was so marked in the Athens of the late fifth century. Thucydides states his policy as regards speeches in one of the most famous passages in Book 1 (see above, pp. 27-8). It is notoriously difficult to interpret:

> As for the speeches that were made by the different parties, either before the war or when they were involved in it, it has been difficult both for me – in the case of the speeches I heard myself – and for those who informed me about speeches made elsewhere, to remember precisely what was said. But I have put things in accordance with what I thought each speaker would have said given what was required in the situation, keeping as close as possible to the general gist of what was actually said.   (1.22.1)

This passage seems to mean that, while not departing drastically from the overall argument of the speaker, Thucydides felt himself at liberty to put into the mouths of his speakers the words which he thinks that they 'would have' said. This is, of course, highly ambiguous; quite how much liberty he considered this afforded is not made clear. We have already seen how Herodotos used fictionalised speeches, such as the Constitutional Debate of his Book 3, to explore themes which he considered important in his work as a whole (see above, p. 20). Thucydides is probably claiming here that he uses less freedom to invent speeches than Herodotos did, but what strikes us, paradoxically, is that he allows himself any room at all for free composition.

For Thucydides, then, as for later historians, speeches served as vehicles for the author's own musings on the nature of power, of war, and of human nature. In Book 1, he puts into the mouth of the Corinthian envoys to Sparta a speech which analyses the different characters of the two protagonists: the Athenians as quick-witted, energetic and ambitious, the Spartans as conservative, isolationist and cautious (1.68-71). The analysis, although set dramatically in a specific event in 432 BC, provides the reader, by way of introduction, with a generalised thought-provoking exploration of the characteristics of the two sides. In other words, whatever its reliability as a record of what was actually said – a question which of necessity must remain unanswered – the speech serves a purpose in Thucydides' literary construction of the war, preparing the reader for the characteristics and themes which he or she will see worked out in the course of the war.

Later in Book 1 Thucydides puts into Perikles' mouth a speech supposedly given at the occasion of the public funeral of those who died in the first year of the war. The speech, often known as the Funeral Speech or *Epitaphios*, is justly famous. But we cannot be sure how much of it goes back to the original words of Perikles. There were probably many similar public funerals, complete with speeches over the dead, perhaps every year of the war. But Thucydides has selected this one, or perhaps more likely distilled into this one elements from several speeches, in order to present and explore an idealised picture of pre-war Athens and of the leader at its head: an Athens that will before long be ruined both physically and morally by the disastrous war on which it was embarking. This excerpt gives a flavour of the speech:

> For we love beauty without being extravagant and we love wisdom
> without becoming soft .... In brief, then, I say that our city as a whole
> is an education for Greece, and it seems to me that each individual

amongst us could with grace and dexterity adapt himself to the most varied forms of activity. This is not a boast inspired by the occasion, but factual truth; the actual power of our city, which we attained through these very qualities, is proof of that ...   (2.40-1)

Immediately after the Funeral Speech Thucydides describes at length the coming of the great plague to Athens and the suffering and destruction of traditional morality that it brought. The plague raged in Athens for at least four years, but Thucydides has placed the description of the plague directly after the funeral speech. This deliberate ordering brings out clearly the destruction of war, and might even suggest to a contemporary reader that peculiarly 'tragic' plot, in which pride is followed by a fall. We have already noted how Herodotos structured his history around such repeated cycles of *hybris* and *nemesis* (see above, pp. 21-4).

Indeed, the very scale of the destruction wrought by the war is one of Thucydides' key themes, emphasised at the outset and remarked upon frequently. He is at pains in particular to show the bloody divisions and the moral collapse which the war brought to those cities, great and small, which were caught up in it. This is especially clear in Thucydides' long description of the civil war in Kerkyra in Book 3, which followed upon Athenian intervention there (3.81-4). Kerkyra was one of many cities which were sucked into the super-power conflict and became prey to factional fighting and internecine struggle of the most brutal kind. The breakdown of law and order in Kerkyra, however, is described at great length by Thucydides, out of all proportion to its importance for the course of the war (except perhaps to show why neither side got the benefit of its sizeable navy). But Thucydides seems to have focused on events at Kerkyra in order for them to serve as a representative example of the destructiveness of the war.

As well as the physical destructiveness of the war, the Kerkyran episode brings out the way in which the conflict destroyed commonly accepted standards of morality: bloody massacres, fathers killing sons, temples desecrated, oaths broken. This erosion of commonly accepted values, along with the actual language of morality, is nowhere clearer than in the so-called Melian Dialogue in Book 5 (5.85-113), which exposes the harsh realities of power. The small island of Melos had found itself in a difficult position. Although it had cultural, linguistic and probably political ties with Sparta, its geographical position in the Aegean placed it within what Athens considered its own sphere of influence. It had managed to remain neutral throughout the period of Athenian domination in the Aegean, but in 416 BC an Athenian fleet arrived and demanded its submission. The

Melians attempted resistance and, predictably, were overwhelmed; the male inhabitants were executed and the women and children sold as slaves. It was just one incident of many such that took place in the war, but it is treated at length by Thucydides who seems to use it as an example of the violence and naked imperialism that the war brought about. Thucydides even reconstructs the negotiations between the two sides in the form of a dialogue. The arguments that he puts into the Athenians' mouths rely simply on their superior military power rather than on any moral claims: while the Melians appeal to principles of justice, the Athenians reply simply that they are the stronger and the Melians must submit. Many have seen, therefore, in the Melian Dialogue an exposure of what Thucydides might have regarded as the brutal and amoral realities of Athenian imperialism.

Directly after the Melian episode, Thucydides begins describing Athenian interests in Sicily. Athens had long had her eyes set on Sicily, with its vast natural resources and powerful Greek cities, an important potential asset. In 415 BC she launched a large expedition to bring the island on to her side. Books 6 and 7 of Thucydides' history, perhaps the most polished and dramatic section of the whole work, are taken up with this Sicilian Expedition. After a geographical and ethnographic description of Sicily *à la* Herodotos, Thucydides brings out the unrealistic hopes, greed and passion (*eros*) for further conquest which drove the Athenian Assembly to vote for the expedition. We then follow its fate from its first arriving in Italian waters, through the long siege of Syracuse to the final massacre of Athenian forces in the rout. It is no coincidence that Thucydides constructs his history in such a way that his narrative of Athens' disastrous Sicilian expedition follows immediately upon her unprovoked attack on Melos: the pattern of *hybris* followed by *nemesis* would have been well understood by his audience. Thucydides' narrative concludes:

> This event turned out to be the greatest of all that happened in the course of this war, and was, in my opinion, the greatest of all Greek events of which we have heard. It was most splendid for the victors and most disastrous for those who were destroyed. For they were completely defeated in every respect and suffered heavily in every way; they met, as the saying goes, with utter destruction. Their land force and ships and everything perished, and few out of many returned home. This is what happened concerning Sicily.
>
> (7.87.5-6)

Athens' disastrous Sicilian Expedition, narrated so dramatically by

Thucydides, with its evocation of the pride and over-confidence of the Athenians in this their greatest imperial adventure, its analysis of the destructive squabbling at home which led to the recall of its most important commander, Alkibiades, and of the depressive lethargy of Nikias, who ended up in command, provides much that is both stimulating and disturbing. For all his admirable awareness of the problems of eye-witnesses, his concern for causation and objectivity, his rejection of hearsay in favour of what can be verified, what remains most impressive in Thucydides' work is its ability to capture and distil the dilemmas, the tensions, sufferings and temptations, which politics and war bring. His work provides the reader with insights into the workings of power, the relations between cities, and the dangers of caution or over-confidence: timeless truths, applicable in all ages. Indeed Thucydides himself expresses the wish that his history would be 'useful' to future ages, that it will be, as he puts it, 'a possession for all time':

> And it may well be that the non-fabulous nature of my narrative will seem less entertaining for the listener. But it will be enough if it is judged useful by anyone who wants a clear view both of the events which have happened and of those which one day, human nature being what it is, will happen again in the same or a similar way. My narrative has been composed not so much as a prize performance for immediate hearing but as a possession for all time.   (1.22.4)

Herodotos had claimed a commemorative function for his history, and had certainly also intended it to be appealing and entertaining. Thucydides, however, stresses the usefulness of his work. This notion – that a written account of past events could *benefit* the reader, and not merely *entertain* him – was to be very influential. It rests, as is clear from this passage, on the assumption that the same basic patterns will repeat themselves, or at least that the statesman will find himself faced with the same dilemmas. For later ancient writers, as we shall see, the usefulness of history was to lie in the teaching of moral lessons, lessons about right and wrong conduct. But for Thucydides the focus is more narrowly political. The individual is largely absent; the real protagonists of his narrative are the city-states, especially Athens and Sparta; even important figures like Perikles or Alkibiades hardly emerge as individual personages, but are rather representatives of their states and their age. Accordingly, the 'usefulness' of his history which Thucydides proclaims is almost certainly to be seen in terms of lessons about the way states behave, wars are won and lost, foreign wars overflow into internal strife. His narrative of the Peloponnesian War would serve as a model for the workings of power and inter-state relations in general, for the destruction caused by war and civil strife: the kinds of thing, in short, which, 'human nature being what it is, will happen again in the same or a similar way'.

Chapter 4

Fourth-century historians

The fifth century BC produced two great historians, Herodotos and Thucydides. Their work rapidly became classics and influenced all the writers of history that followed. As a result of this classic status the texts of Herodotos and Thucydides have survived to us in full, being copied and recopied by generations of scribes from antiquity through to the first printed editions in the sixteenth century. But the texts of the later historians, who tended to see themselves as following in the tradition of one or other of the two, have been much less fortunate. In many cases these historians are now merely names, occasionally collections of quotations in later authors ('fragments'), and rarely anything approaching complete texts. The standard collection of the 'fragments' of lost historians, F. Jacoby's *Die Fragmente der griechischen Historiker* (*FGrH*), contains references to and quotations from literally hundreds of lost authors; often little more than their names has survived. One Athenian author, however, of the generation after Thucydides, bucks this trend. He was fortunate in being valued in antiquity, as in later ages, for his clear and simple Attic Greek, and so has survived in full: Xenophon.

Xenophon

'After these events, not many days later, Thymochares came from Athens with a few ships …'. With these words begins **Xenophon**'s *Hellenika* ('Greek Affairs'). There is no prologue and the narrative picks up roughly where Thucydides left off in 411 BC. So Xenophon clearly intended his work to be seen as a continuation of Thucydides. An Athenian, a generation younger than Thucydides, and a pupil of the philosopher Sokrates, Xenophon experienced the political turmoil of coup and counter-coup that gripped Athens after its fall to Sparta in 404 BC. Soon afterwards he enlisted, like so many other Greeks in the aftermath of the Peloponnesian War, in the mercenary army of Cyrus, pretender to the Persian throne. Upon the defeat of Cyrus, deep in Asia, Xenophon led the Greek survivors in a hazardous march overland back to the coast of the Black Sea, a feat he later described in his exciting travelogue-cum-military narrative known as the *Anabasis*, or 'Journey Inland', an early example of memoir-literature. On his arrival back in Greek lands, Xenophon took service with the Spartan army and became an associate and admirer of the Spartan king Agesilaos, on whose staff Xenophon served both against the Persians in Asia and against his own country at the Battle of Koroneia in 394 BC. At this time or earlier he was, not surprisingly, banished from Athens and settled on lands granted to him by the Spartans. Towards the end of his life, he seems to have been granted some sort of reconciliation with Athens, his native city.

Xenophon wrote a number of different literary works, many of them pioneering in terms of their content and type. Amongst the most notable is the *Education of Cyrus* (*Kyropaideia*) a novelistic reconstruction of the childhood and training of the great king Cyrus I of Persia. It is a kind of study in leadership, and was to influence later theoretical works on kingship as well as the development of the novel. Also influential was his *Agesilaos*, an *enkomion* or praise-speech, aimed at lauding the supposed virtues and achievements of the Spartan king under whom he served. The *Agesilaos* includes large sections of narrative, but all is aimed at presenting the subject in as good a light as possible; there is not even a claim of objectivity here. Xenophon also wrote his *Memorabilia* (or *Reminiscences of Sokrates*) – an interesting collection of conversations supposedly held by the philosopher Sokrates, which tends to be compared rather unfavourably, and perhaps unfairly, with the works of Plato.

We have already had cause to mention Xenophon's autobiographical work, the *Anabasis*, but it is on his narrative history, the *Hellenika* that we will concentrate here. It seems to have been written in two parts. The first part (1.1-2.3) completes the story of the Peloponnesian War from roughly where Thucydides had left it in 411 BC, down to the surrender of Athens and Samos and the knocking down of the Long Walls in 404:

> So Theramenes and his fellow-ambassadors brought this proposal back to Athens. As they were entering the city, a great crowd gathered around them, fearful that they had returned without achieving anything. For there was no longer any room for delay, because of the number who were dying of starvation. The next day the negotiators reported the terms on which the Spartans were willing to make peace .... After this Lysander [the Spartan admiral] began to sail into Peiraieus, and the exiles to return, and they began tearing down the walls with great enthusiasm to the music of flute girls, thinking that that day was the beginning of freedom for Greece.
>
> (2.2.21-3).

The longer second section of the *Hellenika* (2.3-7.5), which was probably written somewhat later, narrates the fortunes of Athens and Sparta in the decades after the war. It traces the growing opposition to Spartan dominance amongst her former allies, which reached its fulfilment in her humiliation at the hands of Thebes, the new ascendant power, at the Battle of Leuktra in 371 BC. The *Hellenika* ends, or rather fizzles out, with the Battle of Mantineia in 362, fought between, on the one hand, a coalition of Sparta and various allies, including Athens, and, on the other, Thebes and her allies. It ended in stalemate:

> Following the battle, confusion and turmoil became even greater throughout Greece than before. I am going to conclude my narrative at this point. Perhaps someone else will concern himself with what happened after these events.   (7.5.27)

The final words ('after these events') link back to the identical words at the beginning of the work and provide both a sense of ending, of having come full circle, and a sense that history never ends, that someone else will now continue where Xenophon left off, just as he had continued Thucydides.

Xenophon certainly intended, then, to be seen as a successor of Thucydides, and it is clear that the *Hellenika* owes much to Thucydides' conception of history. The subject is war and politics and the focus is confined to the Greek world, as its name implies, and particularly to Athens and Sparta: contrast Herodotos' much wider scope, both geographically and thematically. The Thucydidean system of dating by summers and winters is continued, at least in the first section, and, as in Thucydides, formal speeches punctuate the narrative. Xenophon also follows Thucydides' stance of detached objectivity: sources are hardly ever mentioned or discussed, and the personal involvement of the author in the events he is describing – even those in which he actually took part – is played down: contrast again Herodotos' willingness to discuss his sources of information, to point out what he himself has or has not seen, and to cite alternative versions (see above, pp. 16-17).

We have already seen that Thucydides' apparent objectivity and omniscience should not lead us to idealise him as a model or 'scientific' historian. Few people have been tempted to make this mistake with Xenophon, as his history is riddled with obvious gaps and biased presentations. At the heart of this bias lies Xenophon's manifest partiality to Sparta in general and to Agesilaos in particular, and his consequent hostility to Thebes. The extent of this bias becomes immediately apparent when Xenophon's narrative is compared with what we know from other sources. For example, in the years immediately following the end of the Peloponnesian War, Sparta acted so high-handedly that by 395 BC she was faced with a hostile coalition in which not only Athens, but also her former allies Elis, Corinth and the Boiotian League took part: a diplomatic disaster for Sparta and a foretaste of what was to come. Xenophon fails utterly to mention this alliance, and prefers to present the so-called Corinthian War merely as a contest between a righteous Sparta and a troublesome Thebes. Nor two decades further on does he mention the foundation in 378 BC of Athens' fourth-century empire, the 'Second Confederacy', the basis of which was a wide-spread fear of Spartan aggression. Most strikingly, he does not explain the meteoric rise of Thebes in these early decades of the fourth century, and manages to go almost without mentioning at all Epameinondas and Pelopidas, the architects of Thebes' incredible success. After Sparta's humiliation at Leuktra in 371 BC, Xenophon plays down the collapse of her power and influence, and minimises Agesilaos' responsibility. Characteristically, he fails to mention, except much later and in passing, the result of Leuktra and perhaps the most significant event of the first half of the fourth century: the liberation of Messenia, which had been for centuries under Spartan control and the source of much of her agricultural wealth, and its foundation as a new city-state. Sparta would never recover.

The *Hellenika* is in many ways, then, an apologetic for the Sparta which Xenophon admired so much. There is little here of the thought-provoking political analysis which is such an important part of Thucydides' work. His explanation for the defeat at Leuktra, possibly in accordance with official Spartan doctrine, is divine retribution, but divine retribution not for Spartan policy as a whole but for the act of an individual Spartan officer who some years earlier had seized the Theban acropolis without warning and in peace-time in violation of the conventions of war (382 BC). Xenophon, while seeing this act as bringing divine punishment, presents it unconvincingly as uncharacteristic of Spartan policy as a whole:

> Now one could mention many other examples, among both Greeks and barbarians, to show that the gods are not indifferent to the impious or to those who do wicked things; but here I will speak only of the case which is before me. For the Spartans, who had sworn that they would leave the cities independent and had then seized the acropolis of Thebes, were punished by the very men, acting alone, whom they had wronged – although before that time they had never been conquered by any people on earth. As for those among the

Thebans who had led the Spartans on to the acropolis and had wanted the city to be in enslavement to them in order that they might rule as tyrants themselves, just seven of the Theban exiles were enough to destroy their regime. I shall now narrate how this happened ...   (5.4.1)

This appeal to divine intervention as an explanation for human events is reminiscent of Herodotos and fundamentally opposed to the rational spirit of Thucydides. It is true that the latter constructed his narrative to highlight what we might call moral or tragic patterns: we have noted the highlighting of Athens' aggressive imperialism in the Melian Dialogue, which is suggestively placed before the narrative of the disastrous Sicilian expedition. But the gods are never invoked by Thucydides as an explanatory factor. Doubtless Xenophon's use of divine causation should not be exaggerated; it does not appear at all frequently in the *Hellenika*, and not at all in the first section. But the passage cited does reveal a lack of critical thought, of investigative spirit, coupled with a bias towards Sparta. In fact, it would be left to Aristotle (384-322 BC), writing a couple of generations later, to put forward a rational theory to explain the sudden disintegration of Spartan power. He argued in the *Politics* that Spartan collapse could be traced to a number of factors in her internal social organisation, such as laws of inheritance and property which deprived her of manpower (1269a-1271b): a reminder that other types of writing were emerging which were to influence and be influenced by narrative history.

Xenophon's vision of the past was a profoundly moral and moralising one. While he follows Thucydides in his concentration on politics and war, he gives a good deal more attention to the individual commander. For him, as for many later historians, the usefulness of history lay in its placing before the reader individual acts of virtue and vice, of courage, cowardice, piety, irreligion, which might then provide models for individual readers to imitate or avoid in their own lives. Thus in describing the good send-off which the Spartan commander Teleutias received from his troops on his recall to Sparta in 389 BC, Xenophon directly addresses his reader:

Now I am aware that I am not describing here anything which cost a lot of money or was very dangerous, or any memorable stratagem. But by Zeus, it seems to me well worth a man's while to consider what sort of conduct it was that enabled Teleutias to inspire such feelings in the men he commanded. For this is the achievement of a real man, more worthy of note than large sums of money expended or dangers faced.   (5.1.4)

Eight years later the same Teleutias is killed in a surprise attack when, in anger at the loss of some of his troops, he advances too close to an enemy city wall – a classic mistake. Xenophon draws a moral from it, and evidently expects his readers to apply it:

> From such disasters, however, I hold that men are taught the lesson, in particular, that they ought not to punish even a slave in anger: for when they act in anger masters have often suffered greater harm than they have inflicted. But when it comes to enemies it is an utter mistake to attack under the influence of anger without proper thought. For anger is a thing which does not look ahead, while thought is as concerned with avoiding harm oneself as with inflicting it upon the enemy.   (5.3.7)

The significant thing here is that the moral is presented not only in terms of a military lesson ('don't fight when you are angry') but also in terms of a general moral lesson ('don't do anything else when you are angry, not even punish your slave'). Some readers might be in a position to apply the former; most would presumably be in a position to apply the latter, or at least to think about its relevance. Of course, Xenophon wrote at least two works devoted to the person and philosophy of Sokrates, so it should not surprise us if he was concerned to draw more generally applicable precepts out of his history. It was a trend which was to develop.

Other continuators of Thucydides

Until the early twentieth century, Xenophon was the only historian of the generation after Thucydides whose work survived to us in anything but disjointed quotations embedded in the work of later writers. But in 1906 all this was to change with a staggering chance discovery in the sands of Egypt. Written on the back of a land-survey document from the Roman period, mutilated pieces were found of a fourth-century historian until then unknown. More recently archaeologists have excavated two other papyrus fragments of the same author, who, for want of a better name, has been dubbed the **Oxyrhynchos historian**, after the place where the papyri were found. The text as we have it runs only to twenty or so pages and is so badly preserved that there are many gaps ('lacunas'). But it is clear that this is a fragment of a narrative history covering at least from the final years of the Peloponnesian War down to Agesilaos' campaigns in Asia Minor in 395 BC; it may well have covered much more. Particularly notable in what survives, and justly famous, is a description of the early fourth-century constitution of the Boiotian confederacy, the powerbase of Thebes in her rise to ascendancy. This unique analysis throws much needed light on to a region about which we know so little but which played such an important role in the history of the first half of the fourth century. The style of the Oxyrhynchos historian is dry and matter-of-fact, with careful attention to chronology, rather in the Thucydidean vein. Indeed, these stylistic similarities with Thucydides have contributed in large part to the rather high regard with which the Oxyrhynchos historian is held by many modern scholars. Here is a passage taken from the description of Agesilaos' campaign in Asia Minor, complete with lacunas:

> ... hoplites and ... hundred light-armed troops and [appointed general?] Xenokles, a Spartiate ... [having ordered?] that when ... happened to be coming against them ... draw up for battle ... Agesilaos got his army up at dawn and began to lead it forward. The barbarians followed, as they were accustomed to do, and some of them began attacking the Greeks while others began riding around them, and others began pursuing them across the plain in disorder. When he understood that it was the right moment to attack the enemy, Xenokles roused the Peloponnesians from their ambush and began advancing at a run.   (London frag. 11.4-5)

The account of this battle given by the Oxyrhynchos historian raises a number of important issues. Parallel accounts of the same action, which took place near Sardis in 395 BC, occur not only in both Xenophon's *Hellenika* and *Agesilaos* but also in the work of the first-century historian Diodoros of Sicily (see below, pp. 49-50 and 60). While there are differences between all three accounts, those of Diodoros and the Oxyrhynchos historian have some similarities which are not shared by Xenophon. Indeed, it seems almost certain that Diodoros, in the relevant section of his work (Books 13-14), either used the Oxyrhynchos historian as a source or (more likely) relied upon another historian, who himself had access to the Oxyrhynchos historian (see below, p. 48). Xenophon's narrative, on the other hand, represents a separate tradition. The question poses itself, then, which is the more reliable: Xenophon's account or that of the Oxyrhynchos historian, where it survives, or, where it does not, that of Diodoros, whose material ultimately derived from him? Many scholars have argued that the Oxyrhynchos historian, and therefore Diodoros, should be preferred to Xenophon. But we should be wary of jumping to such conclusions. There is no way of knowing how accurately Diodoros followed the Oxyrhynchos historian. Furthermore, even in the case of those episodes for which the account of the Oxyrhynchos historian himself survives, the latter's dry and detailed style is no guarantee of reliability any more than is Thucydides' magisterial assurance; equally, Xenophon's more dramatic style is no guarantee of falsity. The author of the Oxyrhynchos history was certainly seeking to place himself in the tradition of Thucydides; more than that it is difficult to say.

Two other historians of the fourth century stand out: Theopompos and Ephoros. Tantalising bits of their work survive in quotations in later writers: enough to show us that they were considered highly important by later writers such as Diodoros and Plutarch, but not enough to allow us to make many definite pronouncements. The loss of these two important historians is a reminder of what a small proportion of the writers of classical antiquity has survived the passage of time.

In fact, **Theopompos of Chios** (c. 387 – c. 320 BC) has been comparatively lucky. The fragments collected by Jacoby (see above, p. 39) do allow us to get some sense of the flavour and breadth of his work (*FGrH* 115). Theopompos was, like so many of the ancient Greek historians, an aristocrat exiled from his own land. He spent much of his life in Athens, and tradition has it that he was a pupil of the orator Isokrates. Fragments of three works survive, all in their way significant for tracing the development of historiography (that is, of the way in which history was being conceived and written). One fragmentary work, entitled *Hellenika*, seems to pick up where Thucydides left off and is plainly meant to rival Xenophon's own *Hellenika*; attempts have been made to identify this work with the Oxyrhynchos fragments and Theopompos with the Oxyrhynchos historian, but the two works are plainly by different authors. Several fragments also survive of an abridgement, or 'epitome', of Herodotos made by Theopompos, testimony to the classic status that the fifth-century historians had by now obtained.

But Theopompos' most famous work was his mammoth fifty-eight book *Philippika* (*History of Philip*). This text seems in fact to have given a general history of fourth-century Greece, but its focus was on the person of Philip II of Macedon, who had subdued much of Greece in the period 357-338 BC. The surviving fragments suggest that Theopompos did not pull his punches in pillorying Philip, but it is difficult to be certain how representative these fragments are. The later historian Polybios (see below, pp. 56-60) criticised Theopompos at length for bias against Philip, and so naturally selected passages for quotation which prove his point. Be that as it may, the structuring of historical narratives around the deeds of a single individual was to be a trend which accelerated after the campaigns of Philip's son Alexander the Great, who went on to conquer much of the known world and whose extraordinary career produced a large number of such works.

At any rate, from what we can tell from the fragments, Theopompos' *Philippika* had more in common with the entertaining narrative of Herodotos than with the austere account of Thucydides. The scope is broad: not just war and politics, but ethnography, geography, religion, accounts of marvels. The narrative is not linear, but, as in Herodotos, digressions and flashbacks abound. For example, Book 10, much quoted by later writers, was entitled or at least known as 'On the demagogues of Athens'. This was apparently a denunciation of the popular leaders, past and present, whom Theopompos seems to have presented as responsible for the moral corruption of his adopted city: the sympathies of Theopompos were plainly aristocratic and oligarchic, and therefore rather pro-Spartan. In contrast to Thucydides, there is a strong focus on the individual, combined with an explicitly moral flavour. Take the following passage on the court of Philip II, where Theopompos accuses Philip's advisers of engaging in homosexual practices – a standard accusation in contemporary law-court speeches and elsewhere. Such advisers were known in contemporary terminology as the king's 'friends', and Theopompos is quick to point out the potential double meaning:

> All those of a lecherous or insolent character, whether Greek or barbarian, used to collect in Macedonia at Philip's court, and were known as the king's 'friends'. For Philip paid no attention at all to men of orderly habits, who took care of their private possessions, but honoured and advanced spend-thrifts, drunkards and gamblers …. Some of them would have their bodies shaved and smooth themselves, although they were men, and some would actually have relations with each other although they had passed the age for such things. They used to go around with two or three boy-friends and they would perform the same services to others. So it would be more correct to consider them 'girl-friends' rather than friends, and sluts rather than soldiers. For by nature they were man-killers, but by habit they were man-whores.
>
> (Frag. 225, quoted in Polybios 8.9.6-12)

Of course, it would not be wise to extrapolate too much from a few quotations. It is likely that such passages were selected for quotation by later authors, as this one was by Polybios, precisely because of their salacious material, either because it titillated them or, as in Polybios' case, because it outraged them. Theopompos must surely have included much material of a more mundane nature. Be that as it may, Theopompos was famous later in antiquity for his critical stance: critical both in the sense that he criticised his protagonists and in the sense that he subjected their motives and actions to careful scrutiny. Such scrutiny, the historian and literary theorist Dionysios of Halikarnassos later pronounced, was as searching as 'the fabled scrutiny of souls which goes on in Hades' (*Letter to Pompey* 6.7).

The work of Theopompos' older contemporary, **Ephoros of Kyme** (*c.* 405-330 BC), survives, like that of Theopompos, only in fragments (*FGrH* 70). But it was plainly of great influence in the ancient world and was to be used extensively and with approval by later writers. Rather than try to continue from where Thucydides or Xenophon had left off, Ephoros took a radical new departure: his thirty-book *Histories* attempted to synthesise the whole of Greek history, together with events in Persia, from the supposed return of the sons of Herakles to the Peloponnese (considered by the Greeks to be the first event in historical time), which he places in the eleventh century, down to his own day in 341 BC. The structure appears to have been governed as much by theme or place as by chronology. Each book was devoted to a particular region, and within each book events might be grouped together either in chronological order or because they related to a particular theme, regardless of chronology. It is plain that Ephoros knew of and used Thucydides and, significantly, the Oxyrhynchos historian, but it is to Herodotos that we should look for his most important methodological model. Ephoros' interest in geography and ethnography is clear from fragments like the following, a quotation from the geographer Strabo:

> Ephoros, in the fourth book of his history, the one entitled Europe (for he covered Europe as far as the Scythians) says towards the end that the modes of life of the Sauromatians are different from those of the rest of the Scythians. He says that one group is so cruel that they even eat human beings, whereas the other abstains from eating any animal whatsoever. Now the other writers, he says, speak only about their savagery because they know that terrible and wonderful things are startling, but one should tell the opposite facts too and give examples.
>
> (Frag. 42, quoted from Strabo, *Geography* 7.3.9)

The last sentence is a little obscure. Ancient tradition has it that Ephoros, like Theopompos, was a pupil of the Athenian orator Isokrates, and some scholars look to such passages for confirmation of this, seeing, for instance, in the term 'examples' an item of Isokratean rhetorical theory. But given the paucity of surviving fragments of Ephoros, such theories must remain speculation.

This new breed of history, which covers the history of the world from early times down to the present day, has been dubbed by modern scholars 'universal history'. It is quite distinct from the histories of Thucydides and his successors, which dealt only with the recent past and with the Greek world. It was certainly influential. 'Universal histories' were to be written by Polybios in the second century BC (see below, pp. 56-60) and **Diodoros of Sicily** ('Diodoros Siculus'), in the late first century BC. We have already had cause to mention Diodoros (above, p. 45), and it is convenient to leap forward in time and deal with him fully here. His work was entitled the *Bibliotheke* (or *Library*): a significant title, stressing its supposed comprehensiveness. He dealt with all of Greek and Roman history up to his own day in forty books and attempted to harmonise events in different parts of the world into a single chronological scheme. Although only the introductory geographical and ethnographical material (Books 1-5) and the period from 480-302 BC (Books 11-20) survive in full, Diodoros' work is still the largest extant history in Greek to be preserved from antiquity. His historical skills are not impressive; where we can compare him with other extant historians his account is often confused and sometimes downright wrong. For example, in Book 12 he has the Spartan king Archidamos die in 434/3 BC (12.35.4), but then has him on campaign in the early years of the Peloponnesian War (12.42.6, 47.1, 52.1).

Diodoros' chief value for the modern historian lies in the fact that he had access to sources which are now lost to us. In particular for events of the first half of the fourth century (Books 11-15) he used Ephoros, as we have already discussed, who himself had access to the Oxyrhynchos historian. Thus Diodoros, for all his faults as a historian, preserves for us a rival tradition to that of Thucydides and Xenophon. Indeed for some periods, such as that of 478-432 BC, which Thucydides narrates only briefly in the *pentekontaetia*, his testimony is vital, if problematic. Compare his treatment of the outbreak of the Peloponnesian War, which opens with a cross-reference to affairs at Rome:

> When Euthydemos was Archon in Athens [431 BC], the Romans elected instead of consuls three military tribunes: Manius Ae-milianus Mamercus, Gaius Julius and Lucius Quinctius. In this year there began what has been called the Peloponnesian War between the Athenians and the Peloponnesians, the longest of all recorded wars. It is necessary and appropriate to the history I have undertaken to set out first the causes of this war.

While the Athenians were clinging to mastery of the sea, they transferred to Athens the funds which had been collected in common and placed at Delos, about eight thousand talents, and they handed this sum over to Perikles to guard. This man far surpassed his fellow citizens in birth, glory and speaking-ability. But after some time he had spent a considerable amount of this money for his own purposes, and when he was called upon to account for it, he fell ill, since he was unable to give a statement of the money which had been entrusted to him.   (12.38.1-2)

There follows a description of a conversation with his young relative Alkibiades, who advises him not to waste his time worrying 'about how to render an account, but about how not to'.

Consequently Perikles, accepting the reply of the boy, kept pondering in what way he could involve the Athenians in a great war; for he supposed that that would be the best way for him to avoid giving an exact account of the money, because of the disturbance and distractions and fears which would fill the city.   (12.38.4)

Perikles thus foments the Peloponnesian War to divert attention from his own financial irregularities: plainly Diodoros saw the causes of the war in personal terms, and has none of the penetrating political analysis of Thucydides. But for all that, he does preserve an important tradition of popular polemic against Perikles, which is wholly absent from Thucydides' idealising treatment. It is a continuing matter of debate whether and, if so, when, Diodoros' account might preserve good early sources and might consequently be used to correct Thucydides or Xenophon. However, to view Diodoros as a mine from which fragments of earlier lost authors might be dredged up would be both over-optimistic and short-sighted. For one thing, it is generally very difficult to tell how much Diodoros has altered the sources he takes over. Secondly, an approach which treats Diodoros merely as a mine for earlier writers misses what is distinctly Diodoran or distinct to his age. His history is most illuminating in the light it throws on how history was being written at the end of the Hellenistic era. More work needs to be done on the aims and interests of Diodoros himself, and how much his history reflects a distinctly Sicilian or a distinctly first-century conception of the past.

The historians of Alexander the Great

In 336 BC Alexander succeeded Philip on the throne of Macedonia. Two years later he led his army across the Hellespont into Persian territory. By his death in 323 BC, at the age of 33, Alexander had conquered almost the whole of the known world. He had subdued not only all of the Persian Empire, but had even invaded territories beyond its eastern boundary in modern Pakistan. But after Alexander's early death, his vast kingdom fragmented into smaller, though still sizeable kingdoms, which were ruled over by his generals and their successors: Egypt under the Ptolemies, Syria under the Seleukids, Macedonia under the Antigonids, and so on. The tiny city-states of mainland Greece – Athens, Sparta and the rest – became small fish in a much expanded pool. The Hellenistic Age, as modern scholars call it, had begun.

The campaigns of Alexander produced a great number of historical accounts in the years before and following his death. Unfortunately all are lost to us, although the use of them by later authors such as Curtius Rufus, Plutarch and Arrian (see below, pp. 107-16) allows us to reconstruct their main characteristics. The most important feature of all these works is their focus on the single figure of Alexander. Evidence is too scarce to allow us to gauge just how 'biographical' these works were, but certainly the reign of Alexander and of his successors contributed to a growing sense that history concerned the lives and careers of the great individuals in whom power was now vested. We have come a long way from Thucydides, for whom states rather than individuals are the focus, just as we have come a long way from a world dominated by Sparta and Athens. Despite the lack of positive evidence, it seems not unreasonable to suppose that full-scale biographies, that is, birth-to-death narrations, of Alexander and of his successors were being written at this time. Such biographies, or 'Lives' as the ancients called them, would have been regarded as a sub-set of the larger genre of history, though structured around the life-span of a single individual and with more space for the personal habits and sayings of the subject.

Be that as it may, the early historical texts on Alexander for which we have evidence can be divided into roughly three categories. The first is what has been dubbed the 'official' tradition, and seems to have consisted of accounts of a largely military nature, which presented Alexander in a favourable light as the ideal general and king. The later historian Arrian, writing in the second century AD, mentions with approval the accounts of two of Alexander's officers, Aristoboulos, Alexander's chief engineer, and Ptolemy, later ruler of Egypt (see below, pp. 113-14). Secondly, there was a negative tradition on Alexander, which painted him as a barbarous savage, a drunkard incapable of controlling his vices. No texts of this nature survive, but there are elements of this negative presentation in Plutarch's *Life of Alexander*, in the Roman Curtius Rufus, and in a few hostile references in later philosophers (see below, p. 114). Finally, there was also a more sensationalist tradition, known by modern scholars as the 'Vulgate' (ie. popularising) tradition, though it may have been just as 'official', that is, as much sanctioned by Alexander and his successors, as the more sober accounts of his generals. Kallisthenes, a historian who accompanied Alexander and was finally executed by him, seems to have been an early example of, and perhaps the inspiration for, this tradition. A flavour of the sensationalism of his and other such accounts can be gained from the criticism made of them by the later biographer Plutarch, who accuses them of describing how the sea miraculously retreated before Alexander as he passed on his way along the southern coast of Asia Minor (*Life of Alexander* 17; cf. *FGrH* 124 F 31). While modern scholars have tended to share Plutarch's distaste for such miraculous tales, their significance should not be ignored. On the one hand they are testimony to the extraordinary and unparalleled position of power and prestige to which Alexander attained. But such tales also show us something about how history was conceived at this time. The belief that history should be entertaining and exciting, with a good dose of divine intervention and miraculous happenings, which goes back ultimately to Herodotos, continued to be extremely popular amongst ancient readers.

Chapter 5

Hellenistic historians

'Tragic history'

Exciting and vivid narrative had always been a feature of history for the Greeks. After all, Thucydides, for all his claims for the usefulness of his work, engages in extremely striking and emotive description. Perhaps the most extended example of this highly charged writing is Thucydides' account of the defeat, retreat and massacre of Athenian forces in Sicily in 413 BC. Most spectacular is his description of the emotions of the Athenian army as it watches the Battle of the Great Harbour in Syracuse. This virtuoso piece became one of the most famous passages of antiquity, and surely represents the fruit of Thucydides' own creative imagination as much as the transcription of eye-witness reports:

> For since what they were looking at was near, and not everyone was looking at the same thing at the same time, whenever anyone saw their own side prevailing at any point they would take heart and start begging the gods not to deprive them of salvation. But those who had seen a part of their forces being defeated began wailing and shouting, and by looking at what was going on were more cowed in spirit than the men who were actually fighting. And others, who were looking at some part of the sea-battle where the fighting was evenly balanced, were in the worst state of all, on account of the continuing uncertainty of the conflict, actually swaying physically in their fear, in accordance with their opinion of the battle. For they were continually on the point of escape or destruction.   (Thuc. 7.71.3)

This kind of writing, which aimed at stirring the emotions of the reader, became immensely popular in the Hellenistic Age. Events were presented vividly 'as though happening before the spectator's eyes'; the protagonists were shown going through unexpected twists and reversals of fortune, which shocked and thrilled the reader. A conflict between two rival priorities emerged: to what extent should history aim to be serious, rational and 'useful', concerned with explanation and edification, history which

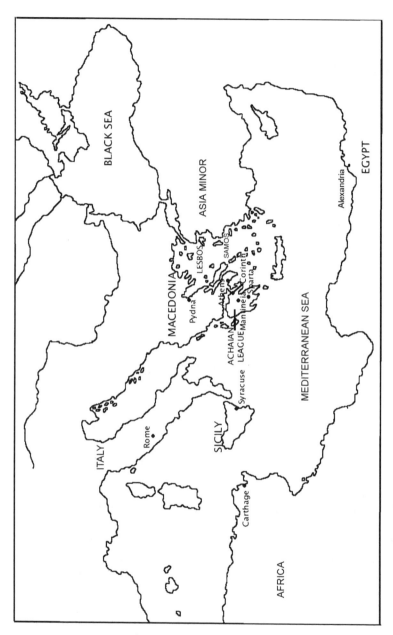

Fig. 3 The Hellenistic world, showing some places mentioned in Chapter 5

improved the reader; and to what extent should it be entertaining and exciting, history which *moved* the reader? Historians who wished to accuse rivals of placing too much emphasis on entertainment might sometimes apply the word 'tragic' to their work, implying that it was theatrical, overdone, and aimed at stirring the emotions. Some modern scholars have tended accordingly to speak of a school or methodology of 'Tragic History', whose aims were fundamentally opposed to writers of more serious history. It is very doubtful, however, whether there was any such thing, or whether historians neatly divided into two groups. Rather, we are talking of two different priorities – painstaking research or exciting narrative – which might be given differing weights by different historians, and which the ancients realised might sometimes conflict.

A key figure in this debate is **Douris of Samos** (*c*. 340-260 BC), whose *Macedonian History* picked up roughly where Xenophon left off and therefore covered much of the same ground as Ephoros and Theopompos. From this fact alone we might expect some attack on these two rivals. Very few fragments are preserved of his work but, according to a Byzantine source, he criticised Ephoros and Theopompos for, apparently, a style which was dry and unexciting ('apparently', because the precise meaning of the passage is debated and the translation given is therefore provisional):

> In the first book of his *Histories* Douris of Samos says the following: Ephoros and Theopompos fell short, for the most part, of reality. For they did not engage in dramatic representation (*mimesis*) nor in pleasing expression, but were concerned only with the actual writing.   (*FGrH* 76 F 1)

On the other side of the argument, the historian Polybios (see below, pp. 56-60), in another famous passage, levels a charge of sensationalism against another historian **Phylarchos** (third century BC). Phylarchos started his narrative, significantly, where Douris left off and Polybios accuses him of putting a higher priority on stirring the reader's emotions than of getting at the truth, and in consequence of feeling free to invent circumstantial detail. His criticisms concern Phylarchos' treatment of the sack of the Peloponnesian city of Mantineia in 223 BC:

> In his eagerness to arouse the pity and sympathy of his readers he brings on clinging women with their hair dishevelled and their breasts bare, and in addition he describes the tears and laments of men and women together with their children and aged parents as

they are led away to slavery. He does this sort of thing throughout his history, always trying in every situation to place the horrors before our eyes. Leaving aside the ignoble and effeminate element in such a treatment, let us examine what is proper and useful in history. The historian should not try to surprise his readers by sensationalising his account, nor should he imagine the possible speeches of his characters nor enumerate incidental details, like tragic poets do, but he should simply record what really happened and what was really said, however commonplace. For the object of history is not the same as that of tragedy, but rather the opposite.

(Polybios 2.56.7-11)

In fact, getting at 'what really happened' at Mantineia is not as unproblematic as Polybios suggests. Certainly, there is good reason to suspect that his attack might not be as objective as it might first seem, nor based solely on methodological criteria. After all, the sack of Mantineia, which Polybios claims Phylarchos exaggerated, was carried out by Polybios' own state, the Achaian League. Polybios had good motive, therefore, to complain that the carnage was exaggerated. Furthermore, as we have seen, vivid narrative and the invention of details, and especially of speeches, was always a feature of Greek historiography, as it was of oratory. Indeed Polybios himself at the start of his work claims that his own history will be paradoxical and surprising (1.1.4-1.2.1); and in fact this very scenario – the storming of a city – was later at least seen as a test case of the ability of the orator to create a convincing and gripping description (see below, pp. 73-4). What we have in these passages from Douris and Polybios, then, is not so much evidence for two rival schools of history as for the different emphases which Greek historians gave to their work, and for the way in which they felt impelled to attack their literary predecessors and rivals, just as Herodotos had attacked Hekataios, and Thucydides had attacked Herodotos. It is to be regretted that so little has survived to us of either Douris or Phylarchos to allow us to pass any judgement of our own, although this lack should certainly not be taken as an indication that they were not as every bit as popular in Hellenistic times as those who claimed to write more 'serious' history.

The challenge of Rome: Polybios

By the time Polybios himself came to write, the Mediterranean world was going through another traumatic change: the rise of Rome. Initially a small city-state, Rome had during the fourth and third centuries BC gradually brought most of Italy under its control. In 202 BC Roman armies defeated Hannibal and the Carthaginians; soon after Rome was at war once again with Philip V of Macedon, who had lent support to Hannibal. In 168 Rome defeated Philip's successor Perseus at the Battle of Pydna and partitioned Macedonia into a number of client states. Although Rome refrained from actually annexing territory on the Greek mainland, it punished those states which it considered not to have provided whole-hearted support in the war. One such state on whom Rome's suspicion fell was the Achaian League, a confederation of northern Peloponnesian cities, which had tried to pursue a neutral policy between Rome and Macedonia. It was accordingly forced to provide a thousand hostages to ensure good behaviour in the future. When these hostages were released seventeen years later, the Achaian League embroiled itself in an ill-advised revolt against Rome. This time Roman power was not so restrained. Accordingly in 146 BC she sacked both Carthage, her old enemy, and Corinth, the capital of the League. Mainland Greece became in effect a Roman protec-torate, and was later formally annexed.

Among the hostages deported to Italy after the Battle of Pydna was the young **Polybios** (c. 200-118 BC), who was from an important Achaian family and had held office in the Achaian League as Cavalry Commander. He spent seventeen years in detention in Rome, but had the good fortune to strike up a friendship with the young aristocrat Scipio Aemilianus, who was to go on to win famous victories in Africa and Spain and was a patron of the arts. Polybios seems to have accompanied him on various cam-paigns, thus seeing at first hand the workings of the Roman political and military systems. When he turned to writing history, his theme was the extraordinary growth of Roman power. He sets out this purpose in his prologue:

> For who is so lazy or apathetic as not to wish to know how and with what type of constitution the Romans in not quite fifty-three years [220-167 BC] conquered nearly the whole of the inhabited world and subjected it to their sole government – an event unique in history?
>
> (1.1.5)

Polybios' was a huge work: twenty-nine books initially, but he later added another eleven, to deal with the period down to the sack of Carthage and Corinth and the annexation of Greece in 146 BC. Of these, Books 1-5 survive in full, the first two books being a summary of earlier Roman expansion. There also survive sizeable excerpts from the later books. In trying to explain Rome's rise to power, it was necessary to deal with events happening not just in Rome but across the Mediterranean world and to trace their interconnections. Already, as we have seen, Ephoros had attempted to co-ordinate events in different Greek cities with those in Persia and elsewhere. Polybios' great contribution was to attempt to write a history which incorporated Rome's rise within the ambit of the Greek world. He was probably pre-empted in this by the Sicilian Greek historian Timaios (*c.* 350-260 BC), whose work is now largely lost but whom Polybios does his best to criticise and denigrate at length in Book 12. At any rate, Polybios co-ordinated events in Rome and Italy with those in the Greek city-states, the Hellenistic monarchies and even Carthage. He proclaims and defends his decision to write 'universal history' near the start of Book 1:

> What is distinctive in my work, and what is amazing in our present age, is this. Fortune has guided almost all the affairs of the world in one direction and has forced them all to incline towards one and the same goal [i.e. Roman domination]. So a historian should in the same way bring before his readers in one complete overview the operations by which fortune has accomplished this general purpose.
>
> (1.4.1-2)

The work is structured on both chronological and geographical lines. The precise dating of events always posed a problem for historians, as there was no universally accepted system. Events could be dated relative to each other ('in the third year of the war') and then occasionally fixed to the wider world by reference to the office holders in various cities, as when Thucydides dates the outbreak of the Peloponnesian War to the year 'when in Argos Chrysis was in the forty-eighth year of her priesthood, and Ainesias was ephor in Sparta ...' (Thuc. 2.2.1). But Polybios, following Timaios, used the system of Olympiads, that is, of four-year periods marked by the celebration of the Olympic Games. Within each Olympiad, he deals with events by year and by geographical region: first those that took place in Italy and the West, then those in Greece and Macedonia, then Asia and finally Egypt.

If Polybios' geographical scope was large, thematically it is much more limited. He seems himself to have invented the term which he applies to his own work, *pragmatike historia*, that is, the history of deeds (*praxeis*), above all, deeds on the grand stage of politics and war. Absent then are the entertaining vignettes which we find in Herodotos or Xenophon; absent too is the dramatic and emotive writing for which he criticised Phylarchos. Polybios' style is business-like and dry, some have even said boring, a fact which may go part of the way to explaining the paucity of references to him in the centuries after his death. Polybios' conception of history, then, is reminiscent of Thucydides'.

Polybios also used another term to describe his work, *apodeiktike historia*, that is, 'explanatory history'. Like Thucydides, he placed great emphasis on the usefulness of history, which he sets against its entertainment value. This usefulness he saw partly at least in terms of accurately investigating cause and effect. Take the following passage:

> The mere statement of a fact may excite our interest, but is of no benefit to us. But when we add the cause of it, the study of history becomes fruitful. For by transferring similar events to our own times we gain the means of forming presentiments about what is going to happen. This allows us, on the basis of previous events – sometimes by taking precautions so that they will not be repeated and sometimes by imitating what was done then – to face with more confidence the difficulties that confront us.   (12.25b.2-3)

Polybios devotes a great deal of time at the start of Book 3, where the narrative proper begins, to a theory of causation. He insists on a distinction between the precipitating incidents which spark off a war, the 'beginnings' (*archai*), the actual 'causes' (*aitiai*) and the 'pretexts' or 'excuses' given by both sides (*prophaseis*). The terminology and approach is reminiscent of Thucydides, probably deliberately, though Polybios in fact employs the terms in a slightly different way. As we have seen, he also insists, as Thucydides had done, on the usefulness of history. This usefulness is conceived not so much as teaching moral lessons, although the mutability of fortune and the corresponding need for moderation in success and resilience in adversity are a constant theme. Rather, this usefulness is seen in terms of training future statesmen in the *practical* conduct of war or politics. He gives long descriptions of practical matters such as cavalry manoeuvres (10.23), fire-signalling (10.43-7), or the importance of preparations, such as ascertaining the correct length for scaling ladders (5.98). In this respect, Polybios' work shares common elements with the technical military handbooks which were being written from the fourth century onwards, such as Xenophon's *The Cavalry Commander* or Aineias Taktikos' *How to Survive a Siege*.

The main theme of Polybios' history is the rise of Rome. He presents Rome's success as the work of fortune (*tyche*), a rather vague term which seems at times to mean something like divine providence, with all the implications that this carries of the inevitability of Rome's conquest of the world. At other times, however, fortune appears to mean merely chance or luck. Despite this emphasis on fortune, however, Polybios in general looks for rational ways of explaining Rome's success. Most famously, Book 6 is devoted to an analysis of Rome's constitution. Here Polybios advances the theory of the 'mixed constitution', that is, that Rome's stability lay in her combining into a single system of government elements of monarchy (the consuls), aristocracy (the Senate) and democracy (the Assemblies), each providing checks and balances on the other. It was an influential theory and marks Polybios out as a major political theorist in the tradition of Aristotle.

The challenge of Rome: Dionysios of Halikarnassos

Rome's conquest of Greece changed the direction of Greek historiography and posed new challenges for Greek historians. Polybios' answer was to try to explain why it was that Rome was able to conquer Greece, and the rest of the known world, so quickly. His history was still essentially concerned with the contemporary world in as much as his aim was to explain this contemporary situation, and he traced the story down to his own day and to events which he himself had witnessed. In this Polybios was followed by other Greek historians who, like him, wrote on a world-scale and tried to explain Rome's rise to their Greek readers. One such author is **Diodoros of Sicily**, who a century later wrote a 'universal history' from early times down to his own day. We have already noted how even for the fifth century he dates each year both by Roman consuls and by Athenian archons (see above, p. 49). But unfortunately his work survives only in fragments after 302 BC, so we do not know how Diodoros treated Rome's rise and her conquest of Greece. Similar could be said about the work of **Nikolaos of Damascus** (born c. 64 BC). He is chiefly known to us for the fragments of his biography of the Emperor Augustus. But his largest work was a 'universal history' which dealt not only with events in the Greek and Roman worlds, but also with those in Persia, Assyria and elsewhere, and which brought the story right down to his own time. But once again, too little survives to allow us to make firm conclusions about how he treated Rome and Roman expansion.

   A striking and rather different solution to the problem posed by Rome was proposed by the historian **Dionysios of Halikarnassos** (fl. 30- BC), a contemporary of Nikolaos. Eleven out of the original twenty books of his *Roman Antiquities* survive in full, with excerpts of the other nine. Dionysios wrote in Rome in the time of Augustus under Roman patronage, and probably knew of the work of the Roman writer Livy (see below, pp.

79-89). Perhaps not surprisingly Rome is firmly centre-stage; the work traces the city's history from its origins down, not to Dionysios' own time, but to the beginning of the First Punic War (264 BC). Most significantly, Dionysios goes to great lengths to prove his central and paradoxical thesis, namely that Rome, the city that had conquered the Greek world, was itself in origin Greek. According to Dionysios, the people of Rome were the descendants of successive waves of Greek immigrants, and her institutions and customs were essentially Greek. Such an argument would have been unthinkable to Greek historians a few generations earlier; the fact that Dionysios makes it now suggests an attempt to come to terms with the loss of independence which Roman conquest brought. By making Rome Greek, the humiliation of her conquest of Greece might be lessened, and at the same time Rome itself conveniently flattered. Equally significantly and equally conveniently, Dionysios stops his history in the third century BC, thus absolving himself from the rather tricky business of narrating Roman intervention in or conquest of Greece.

This twin approach to the problem of Rome was followed by many later Greek historians. By the time we reach the great Greek historians of the second century AD, with whom we shall deal in the last chapter, contemporary history, which brought with it the necessity of facing Greece's present political weakness, was being largely ignored. There were, it is true, historians like Appian who were interested in exploring the growth of Rome's power, rather as Polybios had done. But many historians fell back on 'local histories' of individual cities or regions, in which Rome was only incidental – a form of writing popular since the fifth century BC, when Hellanikos of Lesbos wrote on the history of Athens down to his own time. Or, like Plutarch and Arrian, these later historians immersed themselves in the glorious Classical past: the Persian Wars, the age of the city-states, the conquests of Alexander and the wars of his immediate successors. The age of Classicism had begun.

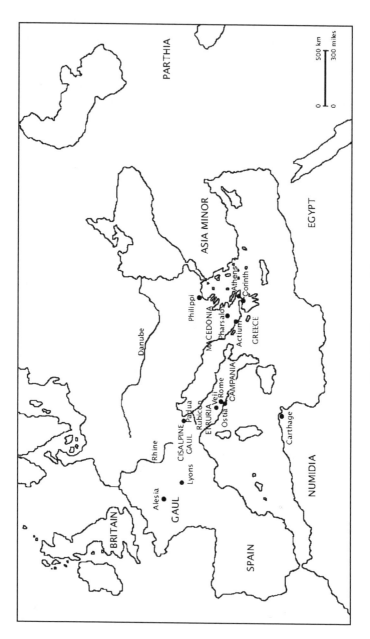

Fig. 4 The Roman world

Chapter 6

Roman Republican historians

The first Roman historians

The Romans had been slow to develop their own tradition of historiography. When in the third century BC they first attempted to write about their own past, they turned not unnaturally to Greek models – but not to Greek narrative history as it had developed in the last three centuries, but to epic poetry. So the poet Naevius (*fl.* 235-204 BC) composed a long epic poem entitled the *Punic War*, which narrated the events of the first of Rome's three wars with Carthage in North Africa (264-241 BC: the 'First Punic War'). The influence of the *Iliad* is evident in the surviving fragments, in which gods appear on stage alongside the great Roman aristocratic leaders – proof of the influence of Greek culture on Rome before any Roman intervention in mainland Greece.

Less survives of Naevius' successor Ennius (born 239 BC), but the title of his epic poem, which traced Roman history from earliest times to his own day, is significant: the *Annals*. This is a reference to the Pontifical Annals (*Annales Maximi*), a yearly record kept by the High Priest of Rome, the Pontifex Maximus, which recorded for each year in minimalist form the names of the consuls (the two highest officers of state), religious prodigies or omens, and any other event of that year which might have had a religious significance, such as a victory or defeat in war, a famine or eclipse. These dry lists, the earliest written records in Rome, were to form invaluable source material for Naevius and for later historians, who used them as the bare bones of a narrative that they then embellished. But the Pontifical Annals also exerted a stylistic influence on Roman historiography, from which it never really escaped: a rather rigid tendency to deal with events year-by-year, an interest in arcane religious material, and a fascination with recording the names of those who held the consulships and other high offices and who tended to belong to a small number of aristocratic clans.

The Pontifical Annals were probably exploited by the first Roman prose historian, **Fabius Pictor** (born 250 BC). His work, of which few fragments survive, narrated the history of Rome from early times down to his own day, culminating in the Second Punic War (218-201 BC). Fabius' decision to write in prose was to have an important effect on the tradition of Roman historiography after him. But equally interesting is his choice of Greek as the language of his work. Plainly, this choice at one level reflects the influence exerted on him by Greek models, especially the popular local histories (this was, after all, the history of a single city). But he may also have felt that the Greek language, honed over the preceding centuries, was a more worthy vehicle than his native Latin, which had not yet been developed as a literary language. Furthermore, his choice of Greek, the international language of the Mediterranean, probably also betrays a recognition of the need for Rome to present and defend itself to the wider world. By the closing decades of the third century Rome had fought off near-destruction at the hands of the Carthaginian general Hannibal, who had all but taken Rome itself in 216 and 211 BC; Roman armies were now crossing into North Africa and mainland Greece. We have seen how Polybios and the Greek historians who followed him sought to come to terms with the growth of Roman power; Fabius and his successors, by presenting Roman history in the Greek language, aimed to provide a justification, in terms of Roman superior virtues, both for Rome's survival and for her later extraordinary conquests. Indeed, by 146 BC, half a century after Fabius wrote, Rome was able to sack both Carthage and Corinth and establish herself as an undoubted super-power.

The first work of prose history in the Latin language was the *Origins* of **Cato the Elder** (born 234 BC), one of the foremost statesmen of his own day and, at least in his public pronouncements, a staunch champion of Roman culture against the influx of Greek practices. Cato's work, like that of Fabius Pictor, traced Rome's history 'from the foundation of the city' (*ab urbe condita*) to his own time in an annalistic frame. It was famous for its terse style and strict moral pronouncements, and for its revolutionary attempt to suppress the names of the generals who headed Rome's armies and to throw the spot-light firmly on Rome itself, the hero of this narrative, and on the old-fashioned virtues which brought her success. Thucydides had similarly played down the roles of individuals and thrown attention on peoples and states; but whereas for Thucydides this was out of a desire to expose what he saw as universal patterns governing politics and war, the purpose of Cato's suppression of names was to glorify Rome – as well, perhaps, as to snub his high-born contemporaries, who greatly exploited their descent from the great men of the past. This moralism, and this self-consciously nationalistic focus, were to be constant features of Roman historiography. Later historians, so often either political figures themselves, like Cato, or their supporters, rejected

Cato's experiment in anonymous history and aimed at magnifying or defending their own deeds or those of their families or patrons. However, neither Cato's *Origins* nor the work of any Roman historian before or after him survives in anything but isolated fragments until we reach the final years of the Republic. As with so much of the work of the Hellenistic historians, so for the historians of early Rome we are limited to excerpts quoted – or misquoted – by later writers.

The crisis of the late Republic

By the end of the second century BC Rome had become the undoubted master of the Mediterranean. All of Italy and Sicily was in her power. With the simultaneous destructions of Corinth and Carthage in 146 BC, Greece and North Africa were annexed, and shortly afterwards Western Asia Minor came into her hands. However, this success abroad ushered in a period of extreme civil strife at home, as rival factions vied for control of Rome's immense power. Rome's numerous foreign wars meant that generals were increasingly in the field for many years at a time, far from the supervision of the Senate, and their armies were becoming personal fiefdoms. The young Marius, a 'new man' (*novus homo*), that is, without the aristocratic pedigree on which the old nobility prided itself, showed the way. Marius came to prominence during the war with the Numidian king Jugurtha (112-105 BC). The prestige which this victory gave him raised him to extraordinary heights: he was appointed consul, a one-year post and normally not renewable, six times on the run in order to lead the defence against a serious Gallic invasion of Italy. But Marius' example was soon followed by other ambitious men, and by the time of his death in the late 80s BC Marius had fought a series of civil wars with his younger contemporary, Sulla, once a field commander in his army, who finally seized sole power in Rome and declared himself 'dictator'. Before his death in 79 BC Sulla had attempted to reform and strengthen the Senate against future warlords like himself, but before long Rome had descended into another round of factional fighting. This time the battle lines were drawn between Pompey, conqueror of the East, and Julius Caesar, whose campaigns in Gaul, Germany and as far as Britain had given him power, prestige and a loyal army. In 49 BC Caesar crossed the Rubicon and invaded Italy, thus precipitating yet another civil war. The Senate officially threw their lot in with Pompey, though many individual senators defected to Caesar. Pompey was defeated at the Battle of Pharsalos in Greece in 48 BC and fled to Egypt where he was assassinated. Caesar installed himself as monarch in all but name, and proceeded to pack the Senate with his own supporters. Resistance to Caesar finally collapsed with the suicide in 46 BC of Cato the Younger, great-grandson of his famous namesake, at Utica in North Africa.

Julius Caesar returned to Rome and declared himself 'dictator for life' (*dictator perpetuus*) in 44 BC, and began to plan a campaign against Parthia in the East. But stability was not to come so easily. He was murdered in the Senate that same year by a faction led by Brutus and Cassius, who were distressed at his disregard for the prestige of the Senate and at his monarchic leanings. The conspirators fled Rome to raise armies in the East leaving Octavian, Caesar's young heir, and M. Antony, his general, a free hand; in the proscriptions that followed, many lost their lives, including the great orator and man of letters Cicero, who was killed as he attempted to flee the country. Brutus and Cassius were defeated at Philippi in 42 BC by the uneasy coalition of Antony and Octavian. War finally broke out between these two erstwhile allies, resulting in the defeat of Antony by Octavian's generals at Actium in 31 BC. Octavian, or Augustus as he became known, was now the unchallenged ruler of the Roman world.

Sallust

It is in this context of civil war and factionalism that Roman historiography of the first century BC was written and read. Amongst the many authors whose names are known, only three have survived in anything more than fragments: Sallust, Nepos and Caesar. **Sallust** or, to give him his full name, C. Sallustinus Crispus (born 86 BC), was like Marius a 'new man'. Little is known of his political career, except that he seems to have attached himself to Caesar's party in the late 50s and was expelled from the Senate for some unknown reason in 50 BC. When civil war broke out in 49 BC, he was firmly on Caesar's side and was given command of a legion in Illyria. Later he was appointed governor of Africa Nova, a prestigious position which brought with it both a large army and much opportunity for enrichment. Apparently the temptation was too great to resist: in 45 BC Sallust was recalled to Rome on charges of extortion. Not even his friendship with Caesar could protect him, and he was forced to withdraw from public life in disgrace. It was in this enforced, though famously luxurious, retirement that he turned to history.

Sallust's first two works survive in full. They are short free-standing pieces, each one book in length. They deal with two episodes in recent history. The first work, the *Catilinarian Conspiracy*, narrates the story of the failed coup of a disgruntled aristocrat, Catiline, who had plotted to assassinate the consuls and seize Rome himself in 63 BC. The second monograph, the *Jugurthine War*, went several decades further back and dealt with the rebellion of the Numidian prince, Jugurtha, and the subsequent difficult campaigns that followed before Roman rule was restored in Africa (112-105 BC). In adopting the monograph form, that is, in limiting the scope of each work to a short and distinct episode, Sallust was cutting himself free of the constraints of annalistic history. In this there was at least one Roman model: a certain Cloelius Antipater is known earlier in the century to have written a monograph in seven books on the Second Punic War, though only a few fragments are now extant. But Greek models were probably more important. Thucydides was the archetype of the close analysis of a single war and the corruption of society which accompanied it. Sallust adopted, probably consciously, a difficult 'Thucydidean' style and the critical attitudes that went with it.

The underlying theme in both Sallust's monographs is the corruption of Roman society. Cicero, who was widely credited with having put down the Catilinarian conspiracy, had famously asked his friend Lucceius to write a laudatory account of his role in the coup (see below, p. 71). Lucceius, perhaps wisely, refused the job. Sallust's work is very different from that envisioned by Cicero. He begins with an extraordinarily long and defensive introduction. Here he defends himself against the twin charges that writing history – unlike making it – is merely a pastime, and that he himself had been tainted by the very vices which he would detect in others.

> When I myself was a young man, I threw myself eagerly into public life, like so many do. There I met with many obstacles. For instead of modesty, incorruptibility and virtue, I found shamelessness, bribery and greed flourishing. Although my soul, which was unaccustomed to evil practices, rejected such things, in the face of so many vices I was corrupted by ambition and held prisoner, young and weak as I was; for while I did not agree with the evil habits of the others, my desire for office made me just as much a victim of the same bad reputation and jealousy as they were. So, when my mind found peace after many troubles and dangers, I decided that I should spend the rest of my life away from public life. But my plan was not to waste my precious leisure-time in inactivity and idleness ...   (*Cat.* 3.3-4.1)

He goes on to claim that he was encouraged in his undertaking because his 'mind was free from hope, fear and partisanship' – in other words, he was not biased (4.2). Although we might reasonably debate the truth of this claim, it is still most revealing: the reliability of a historian was often seen in antiquity in terms of the presence or absence of bias, rather than, or at least more than, in terms of quality of research, accuracy of sources and so on. Sallust concludes his prologue by explaining that his subject will be the conspiracy of Catiline, 'for I regard that event as particularly notable, because of the novelty of the crime and of the dangers which arose from it' (4.4).

A character sketch of Catiline follows, which stresses his vices but also his abilities: 'Lucius Catiline, born of a noble family, had great strength both of mind and body, but an evil and twisted nature ...' (*Cat.* 5.1). Catiline was mad for power, Sallust concludes, but '... he was spurred on by the corruption of public morals, which were being assaulted by two great and contradictory evils, extravagance and greed' (5.8) This sketch sets the tone for the work as a whole. Catiline is certainly presented as vicious and corrupt, but Roman society too is put under the spotlight. Indeed it would be possible to see Catiline, who was 'born of a noble family', as an example writ large of the kind of corruption and lust for power which Sallust, writing in the aftermath of a series of bloody civil wars, saw as infecting Roman society. Furthermore, Sallust spends some time analysing the ills of rural poverty that drove many to join Catiline's army. This is not, then, a history of heroes or villains, as Cicero wanted Lucceius to write (Cicero is not given a leading role at all in Sallust's account). Indeed, as the work progresses, Catiline himself, the apparent villain, begins to seem rather heroic. As the armies of the Roman consuls close in on Catiline and his supporters, he makes a moving speech to his men, telling them to fight bravely for freedom (58). Significantly, the Roman consuls are given no such speech. Catiline, overwhelmed by superior numbers, dies in battle alongside most of his men, leaving it unclear on which side, if either, the reader's sympathy should lie (compare Tacitus' treatment of the British leader Calgacus, below, p. 94).

The *Catilinarian Conspiracy*, then, is a thought-provoking work. There is, it is true, a certain amount of overt railing at the corruption of the nobility, which should probably be seen in the light both of Sallust's own career as a 'new man' and of his subsequent disgrace. But despite this, and despite the confused chronology, Sallust manages to present, through narrative of this short episode which took place over a single year, an impressive analysis of what went wrong in the Rome of the late Republic, and of the viewpoints of the different actors and groups. In this sense, he is comparable with Thucydides, who likewise was able to illuminate wider themes through analysis of single, carefully chosen episodes, such as the civil strife on Kerkyra (see above, p. 35). Thucydides also notably used the speeches which he put into the mouths of his characters as a way of exploring what he himself presented as the key issues. Sallust does this too. The most famous example of this is his presentation of the speeches supposedly given in the Senate in a debate on the fate of some of the conspirators who had been arrested in Rome. Sallust presents side by side first a long speech by Julius Caesar, arguing the case for clemency, and then an equally long speech by Cato the Younger, who argues for the death penalty – the opinion that prevails (51-2). Significantly, Sallust leaves the reader to decide which of the two opinions might be preferable. He goes on to compare the characters of the two men, Caesar as brilliant and ambitious, Cato as self-controlled and austere (54). Once again Sallust leaves it uncertain which is to be preferred. Cato and Caesar were soon to find themselves on opposing sides in the civil war which would begin some fourteen years later. By comparing them in this way, Sallust provides a commentary on the period of civil wars through which he had lived, and which ended with Cato's suicide as the armies of Caesar approached. Both sides, Sallust seems to suggest, had something to be said for – and against – them.

The *Jugurthine War* continues the theme of corruption and decline. Jugurtha, a Numidian, had served with distinction alongside Roman forces on campaign in Spain. But in 112 BC, on the death of his adoptive father, the king of Numidia, he seized power himself, killing one of the king's natural sons and forcing the other to flee to Rome. He kept Roman forces at bay for seven years by a combination of bribery and military brilliance (in particular through the use of guerilla tactics), and indeed inflicted at least one serious defeat on them. Jugurtha was finally captured by treachery and executed in 104 BC. Sallust invites the reader to see in the story of Jugurtha an illustration of the corruption of the Roman nobility and the inevitable decline of Roman power. After another long defence of his decision to write history, and a look backwards at the virtuous men of the past, Sallust continues:

But on the contrary, in our decadent times, it is impossible to find anyone who competes with his ancestors in honesty and hard work rather than in riches and extravagance. Even the 'new men' who used in the past to outdo the nobles by merit, now use secret dealings and open brigandage rather than honourable means to make their way to power and office. They act as though a praetorship, a consulship, or any similar office were of itself glorious and splendid, and were not in reality valued according to the merit of those who uphold it.

> However, I have spoken too freely and allowed myself to be carried away too far by my sorrow and indignation at the morals of our country. I now return to the matter in hand. I propose to write about the war which the Romans waged against Jugurtha, king of Numidia: first because it was long, bloody and of varying fortune; and secondly because then for the first time the arrogance of the nobles was challenged. This marked the beginning of a struggle which threw everything, human and divine, into disarray and rose to such a pitch of fury that civil strife ended in war and the devastation of Italy.   (*Jug.* 4.7-5.2)

For Sallust, then, the Jugurthine War marks the beginning of a process of political struggle which was to end in the civil wars of the first century. The old noble families failed miserably to defeat Jugurtha and were blatantly corrupted by him. This is summed up in the pronouncement which Sallust puts into the mouth of Jugurtha as he leaves Rome after a diplomatic mission in 111 BC, 'A city for sale, and facing a speedy end, if only it can find a buyer' (35.10) – a classic example of Sallust's penchant for the epigrammatic one-liner.

But Sallust's analysis is more subtle than merely an exposé of aristocratic incompetence and venality. There are dark forebodings about the new populist leader, Marius, who brings about Jugurtha's defeat. For one thing, his energy and ambition are disturbingly similar to those of Jugurtha, and the reader knows, with the benefit of hindsight, that he will bring even worse destruction on Rome than Jugurtha did – not least in his conflict with Sulla, who is introduced briefly at the very end as the young officer who masterminds Jugurtha's capture. The book closes with the feeling that the Jugurthine War is but the beginning of the story:

> But when news came that the war in Numidia was ended and Jugurtha was being brought a prisoner to Rome, Marius was elected consul in his absence and Gaul was assigned to him as his province. On the first day of January he celebrated as consul a triumph of great magnificence. At that time the hope and welfare of the state rested on him.   (*Jug.* 114.3-4)

As Jugurtha is brought captive to Rome, all hopes rest with Marius, the hero of the hour. The reader knows, however, how disappointed these hopes were to be: before long, Marius and Sulla will embroil Rome in the first of a series of disastrous civil wars. Jugurtha may have been defeated, but worse was yet to come.

It is perhaps fitting that Sallust's literary career ended with a similar lack of closure. He had embarked on a large scale annalistic history of Rome which began in 78 BC, where an earlier analyst had broken off. But it seems to have covered only eleven years before it was cut short by Sallust's death in 35 BC. The *Histories*, like so much of the best ancient literature, survives to us only in fragments, though the work seems to have been highly considered and much read in antiquity. But the works of two other historians survive from the final decades of the first century BC – the *On the Gallic War* and *On the Civil War* of Julius Caesar himself, and the *Lives of Illustrious Men* of Cornelius Nepos. Both are in their own way unusual. But before we turn to an examination of these texts, it is worth pausing to look at the writing of another intellectual and statesman of this period, Cicero.

Cicero and the theory of history

Cicero is chiefly known for his political activity, and also as an orator and philosopher. But he made several revealing pronouncements on the task of the historian. These are extraordinarily important documents for an understanding of the assumptions which a Roman of this period made about the nature of history. We have already noted in passing Cicero's request to Lucceius that he write a laudatory account of Cicero's role in suppressing the Catilinarian conspiracy (*Letters to his Friends* 5.12). Cicero argues towards the end of this letter that the events of that year would provide material for a great deal of exciting narrative, and especially for reversals of fortune: the sort of thing which had been considered standard in Greek historiography from Thucydides onwards (see above, pp. 53-6). Equally significant is Cicero's plea that Lucceius 'elaborate' his own role (on which, more below). Most strikingly, whereas historians normally claim, as we have noted, to be writing without bias to one party or another, Cicero urges Lucceius to put aside such scruples – an outrageous request, as he himself admits:

> So I repeat my request with total frankness – elaborate my activities even more enthusiastically than perhaps you feel right, and in the process disregard the laws of history: do not shun that bias which you discussed so charmingly in your prologue, if it urges you a little too enthusiastically in my favour ... and let our mutual affection take a degree of precedence over the truth.   (5.12.3)

Cicero wanted Lucceius to write an account which would place him in a particularly good light. What is noticeable here is Cicero's assumption about what the 'laws of history' were. As we have seen, a historian's reliability was conceived most of all in terms of his lack of prejudice or bias. As he himself admits, Cicero's request did indeed involve disregarding 'the laws of history'.

Perhaps more striking from a modern point of view is Cicero's lack of concern about the whole idea of 'elaborating' historical material itself. He sets out his conception of this in another passage, from his work *On the Orator* (*De Oratore*), published in 55 BC. This treatise, presented in dialogue form, analyses the nature of oratory, or public speaking, and the characteristics of the ideal orator. It is itself of great significance that it is within this discussion of the nature of oratory that Cicero places an examination of the role of the historian, put into the mouth of one of the characters in the dialogue. History, then, for Cicero, is a branch of oratory (rather than, for example, being lined up alongside medicine or the physical sciences). The historian's job, in other words, like that of the public speaker, is *presentation*, the presentation of the facts at his disposal in the most persuasive light. The early Roman historians, Cicero's speaker argues, reproduced the bare reports of the Pontifical Annals or other sources 'without any elaboration'. Recent historians, however, like their Greek predecessors and contemporaries, saw the need for a more embellished narrative. It is assumed, in other words, that the historian, taking his cue from the orator, would expand on the bare 'core' of narrative which was at his disposable to produce the kind of exciting and morally satisfying narrative which his readers would expect. A little later, the speaker continues:

> For who does not know that the first law of history is not daring to say anything false, and the second is not refraining from saying anything true: when you write there should be no suspicion of prejudice for or against. Of course these foundations are familiar to everyone, but the actual superstructure consists of content and style. It is in the nature of content that it requires a chronological order of events and geographical descriptions. But in the treatment of important and memorable events the reader expects first intentions, then the events themselves and finally their consequences. So under content you need to indicate whether you approve of the intentions. You need also to make clear not only what was said and done but also how. And when you speak of consequences, you need to explain all the reasons, whether they be chance, wisdom or rashness. You should also give not only the actual achievements of the men

involved but also the life and character of those outstanding in reputation or fame. The nature of style and type of discourse, on the other hand ...   *On the Orator* 2.62-4)

We see here once again the assumption that a historian's reliability lies in his lack of bias. But more importantly we see the assumption that the historian will, like the orator, elaborate on the bare bones of his source-material to produce a more satisfying narrative, complete with descriptions of places and terrain, analyses of the consequences and causes of what happened, and moral judgements on the participants and their behaviour. In oratory, this kind of 'imaginative expansion' or 'reconstruction' was known by the Latin term *inventio* ('discovery'). We have already seen how the invention of circumstantial detail was taken for granted by historians such as Thucydides, so it should cause us no surprise that Cicero assumes its necessity here. If a circumstantial detail was plausible, then it might quite legitimately be added. Such invented or 'discovered' detail was not considered untrue, nor the historian's addition of such material dishonest; rather it was quite legitimate elaboration. Indeed, the speaker in this part of *On the Orator* criticises the early Roman historians for not elaborating their source-material sufficiently.

The criteria for such imaginative reconstruction, in history as in oratory, was always plausibility. If challenged on a particular point of invented detail, such as a speech put into the mouth of a general before a battle, or a description of the noise and terror of the battle itself, the ancient historian would no doubt have replied that 'it must have been something like that' – rather in the same way that a modern writer of historical fiction might reply. Take the following quotation from the orator Quintilian, writing towards the end of the first century AD, who advises the public speaker on how to elaborate on the theme of a city being taken by storm; his words are equally applicable to the historian:

Without doubt the plain statement that 'the city was stormed' embraces everything which is implied in such a calamity, but this brief communique, as it were, has no emotional effect. But if you expand everything which was implicit in the single word 'stormed', then houses and temples will come into view engulfed in flames, the crash of falling roofs will be heard, the unified din made up of many sounds, the blind flight of some, others clinging to their nearest and dearest in a last embrace.... It is true that all these things are implied in the word 'destruction', but to state the whole is less than to state the parts. We shall achieve our goal to make the facts

vivid provided they are plausible. It is even legitimate to add
fictitious incidents of the type which commonly occur.

(Quintilian, *Training in Oratory*
[*Institutio Oratoria*] 8.3.67-70)

Vivid, moving, circumstantial detail, invented or 'discovered' by the
author, was expected of the historian no less than of the orator. We have
already noted how the Hellenistic historian Phylarchos famously indulged
in exactly this kind of vivid reconstruction of the sights and sounds of a
city being stormed, though he was attacked by Polybios for going too far
(see above, pp. 55-6). In the view of Cicero's speaker, this kind of narrative
had been missing in the early Roman historians, but was at last being
included by later historians, under Greek influence.

Caesar

While Cicero was composing his *On the Orator* and musing on the relation
of history to oratory, Julius Caesar (100-44 BC) was on campaign in Gaul
and writing his own account of these operations. Caesar spent the years
58-49 BC fighting to subjugate all of modern-day France and Belgium,
and even made forays across the Rhine and to Britain. These conquests
gave him vast wealth, a loyal and experienced army, and huge prestige;
senators flocked to join him in Gaul or to attach themselves to his side in
Rome. Others feared for their own power, or for the future of Republican
government when he returned to Rome, and towards the end of the decade
began looking to the other hugely successful general and strong-man of
the time, Pompey, as a counterweight to Caesar. It was within this context
of increasing tension that Caesar composed and published the seven books
of his *On the Gallic War*.

Several Roman statesmen before Caesar had published 'memoirs' (in
Latin, *commentarii*), most notably the dictator Sulla. But Caesar's is the
first such work in Latin to survive. The development of this genre was
probably influenced by the fact that, when holding public office, Roman
statesmen often kept archives of memoranda recording decisions and such
like for their own use or that of their successors in office. But in the Greek
world there was a long tradition of memoir literature. We have already
mentioned in passing Xenophon's *Anabasis*, the narrative of the Greek
march inland into Asia and subsequent safe return against the odds (see
above, pp. 39-40). The *Anabasis* was in seven books, and it is perhaps not
a coincidence that Caesar's *On the Gallic War* also had seven books in its
original form (an eighth was added after his death by one of Caesar's

lieutenants). An interesting feature of the *Anabasis* is Xenophon's use of the third person of himself. This feature is even more striking in Caesar's work: Caesar places himself at the centre of action throughout, but unfailingly talks of himself in the third person, as 'Caesar'.

This technique, together with an unadorned and simple style, has the effect of giving an appearance of objectivity to his account. Indeed, some have wanted to believe that Caesar's account is free of the kind of elaboration which we have seen Cicero taking for granted. But this is far from the truth. Take this characteristic piece of military narrative from the description of the famous siege of Alesia in 52 BC, which marked the end of serious Gallic resistance. The Gauls are making a final desperate attempt to break through the Roman lines and lift the siege:

> Caesar now hastens for the sector to which he had sent Labienus, taking four cohorts from the nearest fort. He orders part of the cavalry to follow him and part to go round the outer lines and attack the enemy in the rear … The enemy knew that he was coming by the colour of his cloak, which he always wore in battle to mark his identity, and they could see the cavalry squadrons and the cohorts which he had ordered to follow him – since the slopes and depressions where they found themselves were plainly visible from the heights. So the enemy closed for battle, and a shout went up on both sides.   (*On the Gallic War* 7.87-8)

Caesar emerges unfailingly as the ideal general: brave, calm and determined, who leads his men from the front and wins their unquestioning loyalty. Modern historians of past generations have tended to take this at face value, and to see in Caesar a model of the calm and resourceful professional soldier. But we can be wiser. The picture which Caesar presents of himself is, of course, an elaborate exercise in propaganda, carefully constructed and aimed at persuading its readers to back him against his rivals in the struggle which would soon erupt. Indeed, *On the Gallic War* may well have been published with the consular elections of 49 BC in mind: there is probably a direct political purpose here. *On the Gallic War*, then, together with its sequel, *On the Civil War* (which dealt with the period 49-48 BC, and was likewise left unfinished and completed by his lieutenants) are far from being the straight-forward unadorned 'memoirs' that they are sometimes made out to be. In these works, Caesar carefully avoids mentioning military setbacks, conceals the vast fortunes that he and his officers made, and talks up his own successes. He gives the erroneous impression, for example, that his expeditions to Britain had some kind of lasting effect. But for all the obvious propagandist purposes of these works, they are no less instructive to the historian, both for the main events of the period, for the details which they take for granted about Roman – and Gallic – military practice and government, and for the insight they give us into the Roman mind: in Caesar's *On the Gallic War* and *On the Civil War* we see the kind of rhetoric that was considered persuasive to a Roman reader of this period, the characteristics of a leader which might appeal to them.

Nepos

Caesar's *On the Gallic War* was much admired in the nineteenth and twentieth centuries for its clear and simple style. It was for this reason, and perhaps also because of its assumptions about conquest and colonisation, staple reading in the elite education of that period. The surviving work of another contemporary of Sallust and Caesar, **Cornelius Nepos** (*c.* 110-24 BC), was likewise much read in the last two centuries for the simplicity of his Latin prose style, although Nepos, in contrast to Caesar, has generally been regarded as rather low-grade stuff, neither historically accurate nor with any literary merit. Nepos was born in the Romanised province of Cisalpine Gaul (northern Italy). He played no part in politics, but was part of a circle of literary men which included Cicero (with whom he corresponded), Atticus (a well-known intellectual), and the poet Catullus (who dedicated a collection of poems to him). He wrote several lost works of history, including a three-volume collection entitled *Chronica*. The name is Greek, and means roughly the same as Annals, but the use of a Greek name is probably significant. Not only does it reflect a new enthusiasm for Greek models amongst the intellectuals, poets especially, of the first century BC, but it probably also marks a difference in scope from earlier Latin Annals, which had been Romanocentric in the extreme. According to Catullus (1.1) Nepos' *Chronica* covered all history, both Greek and Roman, down to his own day in just three books: this was, in other words, a work of 'universal history' in the Greek mould. In this he may well have been influenced by the Greek Diodoros, who was composing his much longer multi-volume *Library* in Rome at exactly the same time (see above, pp. 49-50 and 60).

Unfortunately, the *Chronica* are lost, but a portion of another work of Nepos survives: his *Lives of Illustrious Men*, almost certainly the earliest work of biography to be written in Latin. (Some have claimed that they are the first works of 'political biography' from antiquity in either Greek or Latin, but this is not convincing; see above, p. 51.) The *Lives of*

Illustrious Men, published in the 30s BC, consisted of at least 16 books, grouped into pairs. We hear of pairs of books on generals, historians, and poets. Within each pair, one book contained biographies of 'foreigners' – mainly but not entirely, Greeks – and the second of Romans. Unfortunately, only one book survives in full, that on 'eminent foreign generals', as well as two individual biographies excerpted from the book on Roman historians (Cato the Elder and Atticus). The biographies range in size in modern editions from two pages (Iphikrates, Cato the Elder) to twenty pages (Themistokles, Epameinondas, Atticus).

Nepos is certainly not reliable as a historical source for the individuals and periods about which he writes. He makes many mistakes. To cite one notorious example, in the biography of the Athenian general Kimon (2.2), he seems to confuse and conflate the naval battles of Mykale (479 BC) and Eurymedon (some time in the 460s). But despite its obvious historical weaknesses, Nepos' work is significant in a number of ways. Most famously, this is probably the first attempt at biography by a Roman: Nepos has abandoned the year-by-year annalistic framework favoured by the Roman historians before him, and adopted a structure based on the careers of individual great men. In this he was probably influenced by Hellenistic Greek trends (see p. 51). Secondly, Nepos' work, like his lost *Chronica*, seems to have been amongst the first attempts to interpret Greek history for a specifically Roman readership. In the opening words of the preface to the one book which survives in full, Nepos deals explicitly both with possible prejudice against biography and with possible misunderstandings by his readers of Greek culture:

> I have no doubt, Atticus, that there will be many who will judge this kind of writing frivolous and insufficiently worthy of the characters of great men, when they read an account of who taught Epameinondas music, or find mention made amongst his virtues the fact that he danced gracefully and played the pipes skilfully. But those who think like this will generally be people who are unacquainted with Greek literature, and who think that nothing is right unless it agrees with their own morality. But if they learn that the standards of what is proper and improper are not the same for all people, but that everything is judged by ancestral usage, they will not be surprised that, in recounting the virtues of the Greeks, I have followed Greek standards. (Preface 1-3)

Implicit in this passage is a comparison of Greek and Roman civilisation and history. This comparison of the two cultures and the two histories is an important feature of the *Lives of Illustrious Men* as a whole. This urge to compare their own culture or achievements with the glories of Greece seems to have been a feature of Nepos' age, and is an indication of how conscious Roman intellectuals were of Greek achievements. In fact at the very end of the book on foreign generals, Nepos urges his readers explicitly to compare these foreign generals with the Roman generals whose biographies would make up the next book, but which are now unfortunately lost to us:

> But it is time for us to finish this book and to give an account of the Roman generals, in order that by comparing the deeds of the two groups it might be easier to judge which men should to be rated higher.
> (*Hannibal* 13.4)

It is worth noting, finally, that just as Nepos' concern with setting Romans alongside Greeks reflects the concerns of his age, so too do the themes and issues which he highlights. Thus in the surviving book, written towards the end of the civil wars, Nepos plays out and explores issues of contemporary concern, such as the clash between individual leaders and the state, or the dangers of armies not properly controlled by central government – themes which are projected back on to the lives of the Greek and Carthaginian generals which Nepos narrates (e.g. *Eumenes* 8). Nepos' *Lives*, then, may be inaccurate, but they tell us something of the mind-set and the concerns of the age which produced them.

Chapter 7

Livy

Caesar defeated Pompey, seized sole-power himself but was assassinated soon after in 44 BC. A series of further civil wars followed before, in 31 BC, Octavian overpowered his opponent Mark Antony at the Battle of Actium, took Egypt, and secured his power as sole ruler of the Roman world. In 29 BC he took the almost unprecedented step of closing the doors of the Temple of Janus in Rome, an act which marked the end of warfare, and the corresponding beginning of a new age of peace. Octavian, like his adoptive father Julius Caesar before him, had become monarch in all but name. But, unlike Caesar, Octavian now began a gradual downplaying of his position. In 27 BC he formally declared the 'restoration of the Republic', making a gesture of handing back his powers to the Senate, who responded by granting him in return not only huge prerogatives, including control of most of the militarised provinces, but also the title of Augustus: it was clear where power really lay. The settlement of 27 BC should not, however, be regarded as a mere sham. Augustus understood the importance of Republican institutions and traditions. Central to these were the proper working of the Senate and the magistracies, which had been long disrupted by civil wars, proscriptions and blatant political interference, and the maintenance of traditional religious ceremonial. In associating his regime with the restitution of such traditional features of Roman society, Augustus was able to satisfy many would-be critics. For all the harsh realities of power, Augustus must have seemed to many to offer a return to peace, stability and tradition.

It is perhaps no surprise, therefore, that the most famous of the historians of Augustus' day concerned himself with Rome's traditions and glorious past, and represented the new regime as to some extent at least a fulfilment of that past. **Titus Livius** (59 BC – AD 17), from Padua in Cisalpine Gaul, was an almost exact contemporary of Augustus. We know little of his life, a mark of his not having sat in the Senate or played any part in public affairs. But his work was a vast undertaking. The initial plan was to trace Rome's history from its foundation (hence its title *Ab Urbe Condita*) down to Cicero's death in 43 BC in a staggering 120 Books. But Livy later extended the scope to reach down to 9 BC in 142 Books. Only

31 BC – AD 14	Augustus	Julio-Claudians
14 – 37	Tiberius	
37 – 41	Caius ('Caligula')	
41 – 54	Claudius	
54 – 68	Nero	
68 – 69	Galba	'Year of Four Emperors'
69	Otho	
69	Vitellius	
69 – 79	Vespasian	Flavians
79 – 81	Titus	
81 – 96	Domitian	
96 – 98	Nerva	'Adoptive Emperors'
98 – 117	Trajan	
117 – 138	Hadrian	
138 – 161	Antoninus Pius	Antonines
161 – 180	Marcus Aurelius	
161 – 169	Lucius Verus	
180 – 192	Commodus	
193	Pertinax	*civil war*
193	Didius Julianus	
193 – 211	Septimius Severus	Severans
211 – 217	Caracalla	
217 – 218	Macrinus	
218 – 222	Elagabalus	
222 – 235	Severus Alexander	

Fig. 5 The Roman emperors

Note that the exact date at which Augustus' reign might be said to have begun is disputed. Note also that Marcus Aurelius appointed his adoptive brother Lucius Verus as co-emperor and later his son Commodus, who succeeded him. Similarly Septimius Severus appointed as co-emperors his sons Caracalla and Geta. Both succeeded Septimius, but Caracalla soon murdered Geta and reigned alone.

Books 1-10 and 21-45 survive, though there are ancient summaries or *periochae* of almost all the others. We are firmly back here in the tradition of the annalists: this is a history of Rome, not a history of the world. And, except presumably for the last books, this is in no sense contemporary history: it is scholarly reconstruction, history based on the accounts of earlier historians and elaborated according to the author's own creative powers.

Within each book Livy adopts an annalistic framework, thus dealing with the events of each consular year in order, and preceding the narrative of the events 'at home and on campaign' (*domi et militiae*) with reports of consuls and other officers elected, religious events and so forth. But a book-by-book and year-by-year framework would not have been sufficient for a work which covered some seven hundred years. Some larger scale organising principle was needed. It has been suggested that Livy may have structured his books, and perhaps composed and issued them, in bundles of five (often labelled 'pentads' by modern scholars), and of ten ('decades'). The surviving books might thus be divided roughly as follows:

1-5	Rome's early history, down to her victory over the Etruscans with the capture of Veii (396 BC), and the disaster of the Gallic sack of Rome (390 BC). Book 1 forms a distinct section in itself as it deals with the period of Rome's kings and also many of the fabulous legends of early Rome.
6-10	Roman wars in Italy against the Latins, Etruscans and Samnites (389-292 BC).
11-20	Lost.
21-30	The War with Hannibal (218-201 BC). This 'decade' may be divided roughly into two 'pentads', the centre point marking Rome's lowest ebb as Hannibal marches on Rome (26.8-11).
31-45	Three 'pentads', covering the years 201-167 BC, and dealing with Rome's intervention in Greece and numerous wars, especially with Philip V of Macedon and his son Perseus.
46-142	Lost.

It is noticeable that as the work progresses, the pace slows down: the first pentad covers almost four centuries (Rome was traditionally founded in 753 BC), while the final three surviving pentads (31-45) cover scarcely more than a decade each. Livy himself notes the fact of increasing detail, and slowing speed, at the start of Book 31 (31.1). Indeed it would then take another 97 books, all now lost, to cover the 158 years down to 9 BC, that is, an average of less than two years per book. The reason for this is almost certainly the sheer increase in source material that Livy had at his disposal. For Books 1-5 sources were particularly limited, possibly due in part to the loss of valuable records in the Gallic sack of Rome in 390 BC, which is recounted in Book 5. At the start of Book 6, which takes up after this sack, Livy notes that his source material is now correspondingly greater (6.1). For books 21-45, we can see that Livy followed Polybios quite closely, although often supplementing him with material drawn from the Roman annalists. In a classic case in Book 21 he mentions Polybios' accurate assessment of Hannibal's troop numbers (20,000), based on an inscription which Hannibal himself set up, only to put alongside it an estimate from another unnamed source, which gave a much more impressive figure of 120,000 (21.38).

This kind of inflation of enemy numbers is common in the ancient historians; it is seen most spectacularly in Herodotos' fantastical estimate of Persian troops as numbering over two million (7.184). It should be noted that Livy in fact goes on to state, with some careful argumentation and reference to other sources, that the real number of troops was probably somewhere between the two extremes. But all the same this example is a reminder that for Livy the demands of writing an impressive and exciting narrative, and one which ultimately glorified Rome, would often outweigh those of accuracy: the more enemy soldiers one has defeated the more glorious the achievement. In putting a higher priority on gripping narrative and an overall message than on objective research, Livy was, of course, not unusual. Xenophon, for example, had famously played down Sparta's faults; he, like Livy, and indeed like most historians Greek and Roman, had seen one of the central purposes of history as being the teaching of moral lessons. The Roman annalists had almost certainly been equally biased, if not more so. Indeed, we should perhaps be more surprised that on occasion Livy shows himself well able to handle and evaluate conflicting sources. For example, in a famous passage (8.40), he argues that the family traditions and inscriptions of aristocratic Romans must be treated with special care, as they are likely to exaggerate their own role to increase their family's importance – although it must be noted that Livy was not always quick to apply this insight in practice.

Perhaps the most famous example of Livy's sophisticated argumentation and evaluation of sources occurs in a passage in Book 4. Here Livy describes how the general A. Cornelius Cossus has killed the Etruscan king, Lars Tolumnius, in single combat. Cossus then dedicated the 'spoils of honour' (*spolia opima*), stripped from the body of his dead opponent, in the Temple of Jupiter Feretrius. Livy goes on to discuss at length the question of the exact rank held by Cossus when he did this: was he consul or a mere military tribune (4.20)? The issue might at first sight seem rather obscure, but it was of profound contemporary political significance. In 28 BC the general M. Licinius Crassus had killed an enemy king in single combat on the Danube. He too, following the precedent set by Cossus, had wished to dedicate the spoils taken from his dead opponent in the temple of Jupiter. But Augustus, concerned to maintain his own monopoly on such prestigious military honours, vetoed it, although Crassus was allowed to celebrate a triumph. Augustus gave as grounds for this refusal the fact that, while Cornelius Cossus had been acting 'under his own auspices' (that is, as consul in his own right), Licinius Crassus had been merely a pro-consul, and formally therefore acting as deputy to Augustus. Central to Augustus' argument, then, was the exact rank which Cossus had held. Livy weighs the evidence for Cossus' rank, including that of a linen corslet of his supposedly discovered by Augustus himself and which Augustus claimed bore an inscription stating Cossus' rank as consul. Livy seems to conclude that there is room for doubt, but that Augustus' version should probably be accepted. Several chapters further on, however, Livy mentions, apparently in passing, that Cossus performed his exploit as a military tribune (4.32.4) – probably a subtle indication that, for all Augustus' power, Livy wished the question to be considered unresolved and would not compromise his standards of accuracy. Livy was well aware that the past might often be manipulated by individuals or groups for their own ends.

Livy's preface

Livy's history begins with a long preface, in which he sets out his purposes and attitude to his work. He starts by announcing his subject ('a full account of Roman history from the founding of the city') and emphasising the difficulty of his undertaking: both the popularity of the theme amongst historians and the very scale of the task, some seven hundred years of history, make, he claims, his job a particularly difficult one – and, it is implied, his achievement particularly impressive. Then he sounds a note of pessimism:

> I have no doubt that the majority of my readers will derive less pleasure from the origins of Rome and the immediately succeeding period. For they will want to hurry on to reach our present period, in which the forces of a long-powerful people are now working its own ruin. But personally I shall look for an extra reward in this. For

as long, at least, as I am absorbed in those ancient times, I will be able to avert my gaze from the evils which our own age has been witnessing for so many years. I shall also be free of all the pressures to which the historian of modern times is prone; even if such pressures cannot actually divert his mind from the truth, they can still cause him unease.   (Preface 4-5)

Writing about early Rome will provide relief from contemplating the ills of contemporary society: the pessimistic air probably reflects the early date of the preface. This and the first few books were probably written before the famous settlement of 27 BC and perhaps before the battle of Actium in 31 BC. It must have seemed to Livy, as to many, that Rome was still in the grip of a century or more of almost continual civil war.

Livy goes on in the Preface to declare that his attitude to the mythical traditions of Rome's early years will be simply to report them without either affirming or denying their truthfulness (Preface 6; see also 5.21). There was, of course, a very respectable precedent for this in Herodotos (see above, p. 17), although for Livy there is present also a chauvinistic element entirely lacking in Herodotos – Rome is such a great city that it *deserves* to have a mythical past: 'we can forgive antiquity when it draws no hard line between the human and the supernatural, and so adds dignity to the origins of cities; if any nation deserves the privilege of dedicating their origins to the gods and claiming them as their founders' it is Rome (Preface 7). Livy now sets out his vision of the past and of his own history:

I would like my readers to consider carefully the following issues: the kind of life and morality, the kind of individuals and qualities which acquired us an empire at home and abroad and then expanded it. They should trace how, as discipline gradually began to slip, morality began first to creak, next became increasingly unstable, and then started collapsing, until we have reached the present juncture where we can bear neither our vices nor the remedies needed to cure them.

This is precisely where a knowledge of history can be particularly healthy and beneficial, since it provides object lessons (*exempla*) for us to see of every kind of behaviour, set forth on a conspicuous monument. From these lessons you can select out for yourself and your state both what to imitate and what to avoid, if it is loathsome from beginning to end. Unless I am misled by affection for the task which I have undertaken, I believe that no state has ever existed

greater in power, purer in its morality, or richer in good examples
than ours ...   (Preface 9-11)

Various points are striking here. First, this is again a noticeably depressing
vision of the present: morality has slipped over time and led to a situation
where 'we can bear neither our vices nor the remedies needed to cure
them'. It is not clear whether the unpalatable remedies for contemporary
disorder which Livy had in mind are the autocracy of Augustus *per se*, or
whether he is referring to specific aspects of the Augustan legislation. But
what is clear is that the present is projected as the end point of a period of
gradual and increasing decline. This is highly reminiscent of Sallust's
vision of a corrupt Rome. It is a good guess that Livy too placed the
decisive point in this decline where Sallust put it, that is, with the
simultaneous sacking of both Carthage and Corinth in 146 BC and the
removal of any real threat to Roman dominance. A common theme in
Sallust and in other writers of the first century is that fear of the enemy
(*metus hostilis*) had provided a check on the growing corruption and vice
of Rome; once removed, Rome could only sink further into weakness and
vice. Livy's massive history too had an overall trajectory: downward.

In fact, however, as we have noted, this preface was written before the
famous settlement of 27 BC and possibly even before Actium and may not
give an accurate picture of the finished work. Livy seems to have revised
his negative view of the present as his writing, and the years of Augustus'
rule, progressed. If he had adhered to his original plan and broken off with
Cicero's death in 43 BC, he would have left Rome in the midst of an
apparently unending cycle of civil wars. Indeed this was the point where
his contemporary, Asinius Pollio (76 BC – AD 4), broke off his *Histories*,
which covered the period from 60 BC to the victory of Antony and
Octavian at Philippi in 42 BC. Pollio's history, now unfortunately lost, was
very influential and was famous for its Republican (ie. anti-Augustan)
tone. In a similar way, by ending in 43 BC, Livy too would have presented
an overall picture of decline and gloom. The increasing detail with which
the final years of the Republic were dealt with – all now lost to us – will
have added to the depressing tone of Livy's work as originally conceived:
it took some 100 books to cover the last century of civil wars and disorder.
But his decision to extend the work on past Augustus' victory at Actium,
and past the settlement of 27 BC and his numerous foreign conquests, down
to 9 BC, will have allowed the work as a whole to end, one supposes, on
an up-beat note. Augustus' regime will have appeared as a new dawn.
Unfortunately the Books which dealt with this later period are also all lost,
but it is reasonable to assume that Livy presented the Augustan period as

a welcome return to harmony and tradition – just the message that the Augustan regime was actively promoting.

One also notes in Livy's preface a concern with the utility of history, a theme which goes right back to Thucydides (see above, pp. 37-8 and 53-5). History should be *useful*, that is, it should teach the reader lessons. The preface invites the reader to observe the individuals who will walk across the stage of his history and to consider the qualities that led either to success or failure. Observation of such individuals and their behaviour will provide object lessons, or *exempla*, which the reader should imitate or avoid as appropriate. Exactly what kind of lessons the reader is meant to draw, however, is not immediately apparent. Certainly, moral lessons of a general kind are probably included. But the usefulness of history is here couched in overtly nationalistic terms: the focus is placed on the qualities that won Rome an empire and on the sort of behaviour which is useful to the state. Livy may well then be implying that he sees his ideal readers as senators, or officials, administrators and army officers, men actively involved in the affairs of state.

Livy and the usefulness of history

This concern with the lessons of the past is apparent throughout Livy's work. Everywhere, Livy shapes his narrative to provide *exempla*: object lessons of virtue rewarded or winning through and vice punished. As we have already noted, the overall design of the whole work is meant itself to teach a moral: Rome was successful as long as she adhered to her old fashioned virtues – courage, honesty, frugality, respect for traditional religion – but faltered when she cast these off and absorbed the vices that her success made possible. Such a moral vision functions simultaneously at the levels of the work as a whole, of a book or group of books, and of single episodes. This moralising construction is everywhere combined with a style at once smooth and flowing but which is also alert to the possibilities of dramatic presentation – a common concern amongst ancient historiographers. At the level of the individual episode, Livy's tendency to present the reader with memorable *exempla* of wrongs avenged and rights rewarded is perhaps best illustrated by his presentation of the rape of Lucretia in Book 1. This is one of Livy's most dramatic and memorable scenes, and was highly influential in the Renaissance and after. It demonstrates not only Livy's moral vision, but also the value he placed on creating dramatic and gripping narrative: Livy, like his Greek predecessors, aimed to entertain his readers as well as to teach them. Rome is under the rule of the tyrannical king Tarquinius Superbus ('the proud').

His son Sextus has been invited home by a certain Collatinus, who has been boasting of the beauty of his wife, Lucretia. In Herodotos a similar boast had led to death and disaster (see above, p. 19), and so it will here:

> As Collatinus and the Tarquins were approaching, they were welcomed graciously, and her husband, flushed with his success, courteously invited the young princes to dine with him. It was there that Sextus Tarquinius conceived a wicked desire to rape Lucretia; her beauty and proven chastity kindled his lust.   (1.57.10)

Sextus later returns to the house, while Collatinus is away, and is entertained hospitably by Lucretia. When the rest of the household have retired to bed, Sextus creeps, sword in hand, into Lucretia's bedroom and rapes her. He then rides away. Next morning, Lucretia sends urgent word to her father and her husband. They arrive with Brutus, who, it has recently been prophesied, will later 'rule' Rome (that is, become the first consul). Lucretia tells them of her humiliation, and urges them to avenge her honour; with that she plunges a knife into her heart and falls dead.

> Her husband and father were overwhelmed with grief. But Brutus drew the bloody knife from Lucretia's wound, and holding it before him cried, 'I swear by this girl's blood – which was second to none in chastity till a king wronged her – and with you, gods, as my witnesses, that I will pursue L. Tarquinius Superbus, his wicked wife and all his children with sword and fire and all the strength I have. I will never allow either them or anyone else to be king in Rome.
> (1.58-9)

Brutus, thus enraged, leads a rebellion against Tarquinius and expels him and his family, bringing to an end, as Livy tells us (1.60), 244 years of monarchic government and thus founding the Roman Republic. The expulsion of the kings from Rome was a decisive moment in Rome's political history. What is noticeable in Livy's account of it is the central role which he gives to the rape of Lucretia as catalyst for the revolution. He has created a memorable picture of female virtue (as it was then conceived), which would still be considered applicable in his own time: Lucretia could serve as an *exemplum*, or object lesson, of an ideal female sexual morality. But he has also turned the expulsion of Rome's kings into a morality tale of crime followed by punishment, punishment meted out by human agents, but directed according to the will of the gods. The

Herodotean tone – perhaps considered most fitting for this book which dealt with the early history of Rome – is unmistakable.

As we have noted, Livy's moral vision, and his ability to compose exciting and moving narrative, is also evident at the level of whole books or groups of books. The ten books which deal with the Hannibalic war (21-30) show a series of horrifying defeats, all caused by over-confidence and arrogance, and leading to Rome's near-destruction as Hannibal marches on Rome, an episode which forms the low-point of the 'decade' (26.8-11). When Rome finally begins the long fight-back, success is owed to the courage and piety of the new commanders, and the obedience of the lower orders.

But perhaps the most well-known example of exciting narrative imbued with a moral vision is provided by the account in Book 5 of Rome's sack by the Gauls in 390 BC and her subsequent recovery. From the start, we can see that Rome is heading for disaster. First, the Romans ignore a report that a divine voice had been heard calling out in warning that 'the Gauls are coming'. Then they send into exile their best commander and victor of a recent war over Veii, Camillus (5.32). A digression follows, in the best tradition of the Greek historians, on the history of the Gallic encroachment on Italy, which sets out for the reader the scale of the threat (5.33-5). Roman envoys arrive at Clusium, where, after failed negotiations with the Gauls, they go into battle alongside the men of Clusium in total disregard for the rules of war, which, while granting envoys inviolability, forbad them to fight. The Gauls, enraged – and rightly too, Livy tells us – send messengers to Rome. But the Senate, far from disowning the culpable envoys, elects them as military tribunes, thus drawing the Gallic threat on to Rome itself. A levy is hastily held, and without proper preparations or caution an army marches out. It is, predictably, massacred (5.36-7). The Gauls march onward and enter Rome. It is at this point that the tables begin to turn. Whereas until now the Romans have neglected religion, exiled their best commander and acted generally without either planning, courage or due procedure, from now on they do all as they should. They take special care to see to the safety of the statues and cult objects of the gods. A garrison on the Capitol holds out; a night assault is thwarted when a flock of sacred geese, which the Romans had piously not killed, despite their running low on supplies, gives the alarm (5.47). The symbolism is clear: the gods are now protecting Rome. Finally Camillus is recalled from exile and leads an army to the relief of Rome. In his speech after the fighting is over, he makes explicit the moral which the reader should draw:

'Consider in order the successes and reverses of these last years: you will find that when we followed the gods all turned out well and when we scorned them, we failed in everything. Take first of all the war with Veii, which we waged for so many years and with such hardship. It ended only when we obeyed the gods' guidance and drained the Alban lake. And what of this last unprecedented disaster which has befallen our city? It only arose after we disregarded the voice from heaven which warned us that the Gauls were coming, after our envoys violated the law of nations and we, who should have punished that crime, neglected our duty to the gods so much as to let it pass. That is why we were defeated and Rome was captured and put up for ransom. That is why we suffered such punishment at the hands of gods and men that we are an example to the whole world.'   (5.51.5-8)

Chapter 8

Imperial Rome

When Augustus died in AD 14, at the age of 76, power passed to his adopted son, Tiberius, who reigned until AD 37. The Senate made a show of debating the succession and officially conferring Augustus' power on Tiberius, but it was clear to all that real power lay no longer with the Senate but with the Emperor (or 'Caesar'). The years which followed would see a hardening of this concept of imperial power, and the increasing marginalisation of the Senate. Tiberius was succeeded by Caius Caligula (AD 37-41), Claudius (AD 41-54) and Nero (AD 54-68). The Julio-Claudian dynasty came to an end when Nero was overthrown in a rebellion led by one of his provincial governors. Civil war followed, bringing three emperors to the throne in swift succession. The 'Year of Four Emperors' (AD 68-9), as it is sometimes called by modern historians, culminated with the seizing of power by Vespasian, a tough no-nonsense military man and successful commander. His dynasty, the Flavians, was short-lived; Domitian (reigned AD 81-96) outraged the aristocracy by not concealing the reality of autocratic power, and by executing numerous senators on charges of conspiracy against him. These conspiracies may well have been real. The accession of Nerva, in AD 96, and subsequently of his adoptive son Trajan (reigned AD 96-117), brought a new dynasty to the throne, and was greeted by senatorial writers as the beginning of a new era of freedom – but then it is hard to imagine them saying anything else.

Writing history under a monarch with absolute power has always been a difficult matter. Does one praise the Emperor and give a favourable account of his reign, and run the risk of being accused of flattery and toadyism? Or does one run the risk of being thought a critic of the regime and of having one's books suppressed and even being oneself banished or executed? Cremutius Cordus, who wrote under the Emperor Tiberius, famously suffered the latter fate. As Cremutius found, merely refraining from writing about the present emperor might not be enough to avoid suspicion: he was put on trial in AD 25 for praising Brutus and Cassius, the Republican opponents of Augustus. Tacitus describes the scene of his trial (*Annals* 4.34-5). Conscious that his condemnation is inevitable, Cremutius makes an outspoken attack on censorship: Livy, he argues, had praised Pompey without Augustus reacting angrily; Pollio (see above, p. 85) too praised Brutus and Cassius without getting into trouble. By putting him on trial for mere words about men long since dead the regime will ensure that both they and he will be remembered. After leaving the Senate-house Cremutius goes home and proceeds to starve himself to death; his books are burned by the regime. But, Tacitus tells us, some escaped the flames and were read, 'a fact which moves us all the more to scorn the stupidity of those who believe that by an act of tyranny in the present they can also extinguish the memory of future generations' (4.35.5). Ironically, Cremutius' books, which survived the fires of Tiberius' censors, did not survive the neglect of the Middle Ages and are unfortunately lost to us.

The example of Cremutius Cordus and of others suppressed as critics of the regime must have been in the minds of all would-be historians of the imperial age. The most famous Roman historians of the first century of imperial rule are Tacitus (*c*. AD 55-117) and Suetonius (*c*. AD 70-130). But neither wrote contemporary history. Though they composed under the next dynasty, both limit their work to the history of the Julio-Claudian and Flavian dynasties. Despite Tacitus' avowed intention to bring his story up to the present time and to treat the reigns of Nerva and Trajan ('an exceptionally happy period, when you can think what you want and say what you think': *Histories* 1.1.4), he wisely avoided running the risk of being blamed as a toady or prosecuted as a traitor. Both men, therefore, limited themselves to the earlier dynasties, that is, up to the death of Domitian in AD 96.

The approach of Tacitus and Suetonius has been extremely influential in how this period is regarded. But their backgrounds and biases must be taken into account when reading their works. First, as we have noted, both wrote somewhat after the event and, particularly for the early sections, by no means provide us with a contemporary perspective. Secondly, both are metropolitan writers: that is, their lives and careers were spent in Rome, amongst the senatorial and equestrian elites of the city. It was these very groups who suffered most from the increasing centralisation of power and prestige in the hands of successive emperors, or from the arrest and execution of suspected conspirators against or critics of the emperor. The negative presentation by Tacitus in particular of emperors such as Tiberius may be partly explained by this limited viewpoint. It is unfortunate that that we are so reliant on these two sources for our main narrative of this period, as their views cannot be taken as objective judgements on the imperial system. They do, however, give us a fascinating insight into the mind-set of the upper echelons of metropolitan society. We can supplement their evidence by looking to other sources. Archaeology and inscriptions can provide evidence for the development of the provinces, away from the spotlight which Tacitus and Suetonius throw on Rome and the elites of the metropolis. We can also look to the short narrative of Velleius Paterculus for an establishment view (see below, pp. 102-3). Finally we can turn to the Greek writers of the same period, whose concerns were so very different, men like Plutarch, Arrian, Appian and Cassius Dio, who will form the last section of this book.

Chapter 9

Historians of imperial Rome: Tacitus

The works of **Tacitus**, especially the *Annals* and *Histories*, have been extremely influential both in defining modern perceptions of the early Roman imperial period and in providing an influential analysis of the workings of an autocracy in general. It is therefore something of a paradox that his work owes its survival to a single manuscript only. It is rather shocking to consider how different and how much more impoverished our view of this period would be were it not for this chance survival. But this striking fact should also remind us of how much else has been lost from this period and from the literature of antiquity as a whole. There were undoubtedly many Roman historians writing in or about this time; Tacitus mentions a good number by name. These would almost certainly have painted the history of this period in rather different colours; the vagaries of fortune have elevated the status of Tacitus.

The Germania, Agricola *and* Histories

Tacitus was a man of affairs. He was not from a senatorial background, but attained high office under Domitian and reached the consulship in AD 97, shortly after Nerva's accession. He wrote four works of history. In the *Germania*, a text wholly devoted to description of Germany – its geography, the various tribes and their customs – he draws on a long tradition of ethnographic writing going back to Herodotos and Hekataios. As we have already remarked with reference to Herodotos (pp. 19-20), such ethnographic descriptions often serve a purpose beyond the mere provision of interesting or exotic information, for which they were undoubtedly popular. In the *Germania* Tacitus presents a people which is in many ways the antithesis of Tacitus' own and thus holds up, as it were, a mirror to his own society. The Germans are without doubt savage and uncivilised, but they are also uncorrupted by the vices of Rome and, above all, free.

Many of these themes are found also in the *Agricola*, published soon after Nerva came to the throne. This is a laudatory biography of Tacitus' father-in-law, Cn. Julius Agricola, who was a successful general and provincial governor, and responsible for a series of conquests in Britain under Domitian. Agricola is presented as the incarnation of all the virtues of the ideal general, and Tacitus manages to combine exciting military narrative with ethnographic description of Britain and its tribes in this short text in praise of Agricola. Interestingly, the British leader Calgacus, as he faces the prospect of certain defeat by the Roman legions, is given a moving speech, in which he urges his men to fight for freedom against Roman tyranny; Roman rule is presented, in Calgacus' impassioned analysis, as brutal and destructive: 'they create a wasteland, and call it peace' (30.5). The reader is surely meant to reflect on what kind of freedom or peace it was that imperial rule brought to its subjects (see above, p. 68 for a similarly disturbing final speech). But the most striking feature of the *Agricola* is its out-spoken criticism of the Emperor Domitian. Tacitus presents him as ordering Agricola's return to Rome out of jealousy for his successes and he insinuates that Domitian engineered Agricola's actual death soon after. Towards the end of the work Tacitus declares that Agricola's life will show how 'great men can exist even under bad rulers' and that quiet compromise, such as Agricola's, is better than open opposition to tyranny and fruitless martyrdom (42.4). Many have seen in this some sort of *apologia*, or defence, for Tacitus' own service and promotion under the hated Domitian.

The *Agricola*, in its presentation of Domitian as the dissimulating tyrant, foreshadows many of the themes which would be explored more fully in the *Histories* and *Annals*. Together these two works provide a narrative history of the period from the accession of Tiberius in AD 14 to the death of Domitian in AD 96, but in fact the *Histories*, which cover the later part of this period, were published first. Thus Tacitus gradually moves back in time from his own period. The Christian writer Jerome tells us that the *Annals* and *Histories* together, which he labels simply 'Lives of the Caesars', contained 30 books (*Comm. Zacch.* 3.14.47, 1522 Migne). The exact number of books which the two works contained respectively is not known for certain, but it is clear that, although Jerome seems to have envisaged reading them as a consecutive narrative from AD 14 to AD 96, they were in fact two distinct works.

The *Histories* begins with the assumption of powers by that year's consuls in January AD 69, in the middle, that is, of the upheaval of the 'Year of Four Emperors'. The decision to begin thus at the start of a consular year but *in medias res* is both a literary and a political statement, a way both of declaring that he is writing in the tradition of the Republican annalists, like Sallust in his *Histories*, and at the same time of making clear by implication the irrelevance of the Republican facade which the emperors maintained: consuls no longer mattered. The abrupt opening also fits with the gripping fast-moving quality of the story as Tacitus tells it. As Tacitus makes clear in the preface, the *Histories* will present the reader with what one modern scholar has dubbed a 'disaster narrative':

> The work on which I am embarking is rich in disasters, terrible with battles, torn with rebellions, and savage even in peace. Four emperors were slain by the sword. There were three civil wars, even more foreign wars, and often wars which combined both together … Furthermore even Italy itself fell victim to catastrophes which were either unprecedented or had not occurred for many centuries. Cities in the most fertile part of Campania were burned down or buried, and Rome was devastated by fires which destroyed its oldest temples … (*Histories* 1.2.1-2)

The stress on the unprecedented nature of the sufferings caused by the wars and upheaval which Tacitus will describe is reminiscent of the claims made by Thucydides regarding the Peloponnesian War (e.g. Thuc. 1.23: see above, pp. 26-7): this is to be moving, dramatic narrative. But, as Tacitus goes on, this is also to be narrative from which the reader might benefit. The *exempla* provided are of a rather sombre nature, but still instructive:

> However the period was not so barren of merit that it did not produce some good exemplars as well. Mothers accompanied their children in flight, wives followed their husbands into exile. Relatives displayed courage, sons-in-law fidelity, and the loyalty of slaves remained firm even in the face of torture. Suicide, the ultimate necessity, was born bravely by distinguished men, and there were death-scenes to rival the glorious deaths of our ancestors.
> (*Histories* 1.3.1)

It is unfortunate that of the probably twelve Books of the *Histories*, only the first five survive, of which the last breaks off unfinished in AD 70. This takes the story only one and a half years further on. The lost books would have narrated the reigns of Vespasian, his son Titus and the hated Domitian. But even without these lost books, we can see the acuteness of Tacitus' political analysis. One of the themes of the surviving section is that imperial power rested, whatever the constitutional niceties, on the support of the troops on the frontiers. Tacitus characteristically expresses this in a striking single line: 'For the secret of empire was now divulged, that an emperor could be made elsewhere than at Rome' (*Histories* 1.4.2).

The epigram, which contains within it a thought-provoking paradox, is one of the marks of Tacitus' style, and perhaps reveals an influence from Sallust. Take also his memorable description of Galba, who was considered 'capable of ruling, if only he hadn't ruled' (*capax imperii, nisi imperasset*), which is both striking and incisive; it suggests that it is in the nature of absolute power to corrupt all who touch it, and is an insult to Galba specifically (1.49.4).

The Annals

With the *Annals*, Tacitus turned back in time again to the death of Augustus and brought the story up to where the *Histories* began in AD 69. It thus dealt with the reigns of Tiberius, Caligula, Claudius and Nero, and probably the start of the short-lived reign of Galba. The backwards move may have been a result of Tacitus' realisation that the roots of the civil wars of AD 69-70 and of the tyranny of Domitian lay in the early years of the principate, which thus needed analysis. The *Annals* probably contained eighteen books in all, perhaps to be divided into three sections of six books each ('hexads'):

1-6   Reign of Tiberius. (Most of Book 5 is lost.)
7-12   Reign of Caligula and Claudius. (Books 7-10 are lost.)
13-18   Reign of Nero. (Books 17-18 are lost.)

The *Annals*, despite its precarious passage through the Middle Ages, has become one of the most famous works to survive from antiquity. The reason is simple: Tacitus turns the spotlight on autocratic rule and exposes the workings of power and the mind of the autocrat. He sets out his programme in the opening words:

> The city of Rome at the beginning was ruled by kings: freedom and the consulate were brought in by L. Brutus .... But while the successes and setbacks of the old Roman people have been related by famous writers, and intellects of distinction were not lacking to tell of the Augustan age (until they were put off by the rising tide of flattery), the histories of Tiberius, Caligula, Claudius and Nero were falsified out of fear while those emperors were themselves alive, and when they died were written with the memory of recent hatreds still vivid. For this reason it is my intention to say a little about Augustus, especially about his last period, and afterwards to describe the principate of Tiberius and its sequel, without anger or bias – for neither of which have I any motive.   (*Annals* 1.1.1-6)

After this opening Tacitus begins his summary of the realities of power under Augustus. There is an implicit criticism here of imperial despotism, which makes it impossible for historians to write freely of the current emperor or dynasty. There is also here a veiled but respectful reference to Sallust and Livy, and perhaps others, the 'famous writers and intellects of distinction' of an earlier age. And there is the usual claim to impartiality. But what is remarkable about this prologue is what is not said. There are none of the usual claims here of the importance of the subject, no mention of wars or crises to be described, or the exciting nature of what is to be narrated. The impression given is that the period of imperial rule produced nothing to be proud of, no glorious successes, no victories or achievements. Rather, imperial rule in Rome is painted as banal and grim. If Brutus brought 'freedom and the consulate' to Rome, by the end of Book 1 we will see how both exist in name only under Tiberius (1.81). This is the history of tyranny.

This presentation of the history of imperial Rome as grim, depressing and unworthy of historiographical treatment on the grand scale is made more explicit in a section of Book 4:

I am well aware that many of the things which I have related and which I will relate may perhaps seem insignificant and too trivial to mention. But no-one should compare my *Annals* with the writings of those who composed the histories of the old Roman people. They dealt with massive wars, the storming of cities, kings put to flight or captured ... My work, on the contrary, is restricted and brings no glory, since peace was unbroken, or disturbed by only minor incidents, affairs in Rome were grim, and the emperor uninterested in expanding the empire. Yet there is some point in focusing on what at first sight are trivialities, as it is by such things that the great events of history are set in motion... . Now that Rome's constitution has been changed and the Roman state is little different from a monarchy, it is useful to collect and record such details. For few people can distinguish the wise and the honourable from the dishonourable, or the useful from the harmful, but many can learn from the experiences of others.

But, although these topics will be useful, they provide hardly any entertainment. What holds the attention of readers and renews their interest are geographical descriptions, the fluctuating fortunes of battles and the glorious deaths of generals. My account, on the other hand, is a collection of savage orders, endless accusations, false friendships, and the slaughter of the innocent, always for the same reasons – a nauseating and monotonous catalogue.

(*Annals* 4. 32.1-33.3)

Tacitus here skilfully reverses the standard claims made by ancient historians that their accounts will be exciting and worth reading. In so doing he manages to present his own work as novel and, despite the explicit claims that it will not bring pleasure, paradoxically both interesting and useful. Tacitus' focus is, as these statements make clear, on the person of the emperor and on his relations with the senatorial classes. He has succeeded in creating a compelling picture of palace intrigue against a depressing backdrop of repression and self-censorship.

Tacitus' portrait of Tiberius

Tacitus' picture of the Emperor Tiberius is perhaps the most memorable, and also the most full (partly a result of chance, as more of the first hexad survives than of the other two). Tiberius, who came to power in AD 14 at the age of fifty-five, is in Tacitus' telling an isolated, taciturn and reclusive figure. He deliberately conceals his wishes from the Senate and plays a cruel game of pretending not to want power while in reality exercising it severely. For example, immediately upon his accession, he makes a show of returning powers to the Senate, only to be implored by the terrified senators that a single controlling mind is needed. To Tacitus, this is mere show, a ludicrous pretence, the effect of which was to humiliate the Senate further. According to Tacitus, those senators who pressed Tiberius on which powers he wanted to take and which to give up earned the emperor's hatred. Finally 'exhausted at last by the general outcry and by individual appeals, Tiberius gradually gave way, not to the point of acknowledging that he was assuming power, but of ceasing to refuse and to be entreated' (1.13.6). So Tacitus presents as a mere facade what others might have presented as a commendable respect for Republican sentiment: for Tacitus the effect of Tiberius' apparent reluctance to accept the wide-ranging powers offered was to disguise his real wishes and to place the senators in an intolerable position. Towards the end of the first book, Tacitus records another such incident of dissemblance and humiliation. At the consular elections, Tiberius refuses to make clear his wishes as to who should be elected. Once again Tacitus sees the worst motive: for him this is not from any wish on Tiberius' part to have a free vote; rather it results from a treacherous and slippery policy of confusion and humiliation. 'The policy', Tacitus tells us, 'sounded plausible but was in reality meaningless and destined to result in a slavery that was all the more detestable the more it was disguised under a semblance of liberty' (1.81.3).

Tacitus presents Tiberius as getting worse as his reign progresses. Finally he abandons Rome completely and rules by edict from his retreat on the island of Capri, where Tacitus presents him as indulging a taste for luxury and debauchery which had until then remained hidden. In his later years he comes to place great trust in the commander of his Praetorian Guard, Sejanus, whom Tacitus paints as unpleasant and vicious in the extreme, but is eventually betrayed by him. The section which dealt with Tiberius' arrest of Sejanus is unfortunately missing from the surviving portions of the *Annals*, but the theme of Tiberius' increasing isolation and loneliness, together with his secretiveness and dissimulation, is central to Tacitus' presentation of him throughout. Here is part of the historian's final summing-up of Tiberius' life:

> There were different phases in his behaviour too. There was a period exceptional both in terms of his life and reputation while he was a private individual or held commands under Augustus. There was a period of concealment and cunning when he pretended to be virtuous while Germanicus and Drusus survived. He was likewise a mixture of good and bad while his mother was alive, and he was infamous for cruelty, but kept his lusts concealed, as long as he loved Sejanus – or feared him. Finally he erupted into crimes and degradations alike when at last, now that fear and shame were gone, he followed only his own inclinations.   (*Annals* 6.51.3)

A major theme of Tacitus' presentation of Tiberius are the trials of leading senators on charges of treason which are said to have taken place with increasing frequency throughout his reign. Tacitus, perhaps influenced by more recent history under Domitian, gives a picture of a reign of terror. However, this appearance is most misleading. Even when one examines the narrative of Tacitus himself, he actually mentions no more than a dozen or so guilty verdicts over a reign of 23 years or so. In other words, while not actually telling untruths, Tacitus has taken such incidents, written them up at length into dramatic and striking episodes, and used them as a comment on, and symbol of, both Tiberius' reign and the principate as a whole.

Indeed, Tacitus shows himself the master of innuendo. A good example concerns the death of Germanicus, Tiberius' nephew, adoptive son and designated successor. He had a brilliant military career in Rome's northern provinces, for which he celebrated a triumph, but died suddenly in the East amidst rumours that he had been poisoned, possibly on Tiberius' orders. Tacitus uses Germanicus as a foil for Tiberius – a technique well known to ancient orators, by which an individual can be put in a particularly bad light by comparing him with someone better. This implicit comparison of Tiberius with Germanicus is made all the more telling by an extended and explicit favourable comparison of Germanicus with the famous Alexander the Great, which Tacitus presents as the thoughts of the mourners at his funeral and which was the ultimate accolade for a general (*Annals* 2.73). Germanicus is also given a fine death-bed scene and glowing obituary. Tiberius is presented as resenting Germanicus' successes and popularity, in the same way that Domitian resented Agricola's, and while Tacitus never says directly that he believes that Tiberius ordered Germanicus' death, nor does he provide any evidence, such is plainly the implication. When Germanicus' body reaches Rome amidst great popular mourning and attended by his grieving wife Agrippina, this is how Tacitus describes the Emperor's reaction:

> He and Augusta [Tiberius' wife] made no public appearances, either because they thought it beneath them to mourn openly, or because they feared that, if all eyes were fixed on their faces, their hypocrisy would be found out. I cannot ascertain either in the historians or in the official archives any record that Germanicus' mother, Antonia, played any prominent part in the proceedings .... She may have been prevented by ill-health, or her spirit, overcome by grief, may have been unable to face the visible evidence of her great loss. But I find it more credible that she was prevented from going out by Tiberius and Augusta, who themselves did not leave home, in order that they might seem to be grieving just as much as her ...   (*Annals* 3.3)

Twice in this passage Tacitus ascribes to Tiberius sinister motives. In the first instance he presents two alternatives for why Tiberius did not go out publicly to mourn Germanicus; the second is less creditable than the first, and is plainly the one the reader is meant to find more persuasive. This is a favourite Tacitean technique. In the second instance, Tacitus merely states, again without presenting any evidence, that it is more believable that Germanicus' mother did not go out to the funeral because she was prevented from doing so by Tiberius. This is Tacitean innuendo at its most skilful.

The *impression* which Tacitus gives, therefore, of Tiberius' reign is far from objective. But before we rush to condemn Tacitus, we should remember the very different priorities that ancient historians had, and the very different ways in which ancient audiences conceived of the genre of history. The historian was expected to write interesting and gripping narrative; he was expected to provide moral or political lessons – good and bad conduct which could in practice be imitated or avoided or at least be passively applauded or deplored. Provided he did not overstep the boundaries set up by the basic and undisputed facts, he was allowed much lee-way for dramatic reconstruction. Indeed, the criterion for such reconstruction was often what was plausible, or, as Tacitus puts it in this passage, 'credible' (see above, pp. 72-4). Furthermore, some historians, the best, provided an analysis at a deeper level of the societies that they wrote about, of power and empire, or of human nature. Thucydides' exploration of the nature of war and the powers of a democracy to fight one is a classic example. On this criterion, Tacitus' presentation of Tiberius' regime is masterful. His account, which relies so heavily, it is true, on innuendo or on the working-up of specially selected dramatic scenes, provides a compelling analysis of despotism, of how power corrupts and absolute power corrupts absolutely, of how all are trapped by the realities of monarchic rule, even the ruler himself.

Tacitus allowed himself particular liberty when reporting the thoughts or motives of actors in his drama, the emperor in particular, and when composing speeches. We have already noted the long tradition, going back to Herodotos, of putting words into the mouths of characters in order to bring out issues of concern to the historian. In fact, with Tacitus' *Annals* we are in the unique position of being able to compare one of the speeches recorded in his works with an official document of the time which records the same speech. The speech in question was delivered by the Emperor Claudius to the Senate in AD 48, and argued for the admission of Gallic nobles into that body (*Annals* 11.24). By chance, an official version of this speech survives on an inscription from Lyons (*CIL* 13.1668 = *ILS* 212). A number of things are notable. First, the inscription confirms that Claudius did actually make a speech on this topic: Tacitus has not invented the whole thing. Second, Tacitus has re-written the speech in his own words and his own style: indeed, in the view of most scholars he offers a considerably clearer and more concise version than the one on the inscription. Thirdly, while Tacitus' version and the official version do agree on the main points, there are also considerable differences. Scholars differ amongst themselves as to whether Tacitus' version is largely faithful or not to the original, but for our purposes it is perhaps sufficient to remind ourselves of Thucydides' famous, and famously vague, words: 'I have put things in accordance with what I thought each speaker would have said given what was required in the situation, keeping as close as possible to the general gist of what was actually said' (Thuc. 1.22.1: see above, pp. 33-4).

Chapter 10

Historians of imperial Rome: other voices

Establishment history: Velleius Paterculus

But before we leave Tiberius for good, we shall pause to consider one more historian, who gives a rather different impression of his reign and who approached his task in a rather different way. **Velleius Paterculus** (born *c.* 20 BC) lived and wrote in the reign of Tiberius, and indeed served under him on numerous campaigns. His work, most of which survives, is remarkable in its difference from Tacitus' on almost every count. First, in just two books, he covers Roman history from earliest times to the present day: this is a very different kind of account, and perhaps aimed at a rather different audience. The style is fast-moving and varied. Book 1, the last section of which is missing, seems to have ended at the fall of Carthage in 146 BC. Book 2 brings the story up to AD 29. A large part of this second book is devoted to the reign of the current emperor, Tiberius. Here not only is much information given that is not found in Tacitus, but – most striking – the picture of Tiberius that emerges is wholly positive. According- ing to Velleius, Tiberius is the perfect emperor: generous, just, a benevo- lent supporter of Germanicus and a friend of the Senate. Take the following passage towards the end of Book 2:

> But having set before the reader a sort of general outline of the principate of Tiberius Caesar, let us now review the details... With what dignity did he listen to the trial of ... [there is probably a gap in the text here], not in the capacity of emperor but as a senator and judge! How swiftly did he suppress that ungrateful man when he was plotting revolution! How well had he trained and instructed Germanicus, how well had he personally educated him in the basics of military science, so that he was later able to welcome him home as conqueror of Germany! With what honours did he exalt him, young though he was, making the magnificence of his triumph correspond to the greatness of his deeds! How often did he honour the people with largesse, and how gladly, whenever he could do so with the Senate's sanction, did he by his generosity make good the

ranks of the Senate! But he did this in such a way as not to encourage extravagance, nor to allow honest poverty to be deprived of its rank!

(2.129.1-3)

This is very much the establishment, sanctioned point of view. Of course, it would be hard to imagine any historian being foolish enough to publish a history that was openly critical of any emperor while that emperor was still alive, so its positive tone should not altogether surprise us. But we have seen how one-sided is Tacitus' presentation of Tiberius' reign, so Velleius provides a useful corrective to this: there *was* another way of seeing things. Furthermore, establishment points of view are not worthless. Velleius allows us to see how Tiberius' reign might have been regarded and talked of by an enthusiast for his regime. While Velleius' account does not have the dramatic tension of Tacitus', nor is its picture of the emperor so memorable, it is an important source both for the details of Tiberius' reign and for the mentality of at least some members of the upper classes under his rule. It should not be dismissed out of hand.

Biographical history: Suetonius

Much of Tacitus' projection of imperial history is focused on the person of the emperor. **Suetonius**, a younger contemporary of Tacitus, was to press this growing trend towards biography to its limits. C. Suetonius Tranquillus (born *c*. AD 70) was from a modest equestrian background, but enjoyed a spectacularly successful career in the imperial administration, rising to manage the imperial archives and finally to become the private secretary of the Emperor Hadrian in the early years of the latter's reign. He is an example of a new breed of imperial administrators who owed their advancement to the Emperor directly rather than to the Senate and the old Republican machinery. Suetonius was rumoured to have been dismissed in disgrace from his position by Hadrian for some misdemeanour unknown to us, and certainly from AD 122 we hear nothing more about him. It is unclear what exactly happened.

Suetonius had a wide range of scholarly interests. His first foray into biography declares the influence of Nepos in its very title, the *Lives of Illustrious Men* (see above, pp. 76-8). This collection consisted of a series of short biographies of literary figures, of which just a small section on grammarians and orators survives. But Suetonius' most famous work, indeed for centuries one of the most influential works in the Latin language, was his series of imperial biographies, the *Lives of the Caesars*. There are twelve biographies, grouped probably into two books, and beginning with Julius Caesar. The collection ends at the same point as Tacitus' *Histories*, that is, with the death of Domitian and before the reigning emperor's dynasty came to power.

The focus is most definitely on the individual emperors themselves; wider events outside Rome are hardly treated. The reason for this concentration on the person of the emperor, which is discernible to an extent in Tacitus too, is not hard to find: in an age of increasing monopoly of power by the emperors, to write history meant increasingly to write biography, or at least throw the spotlight on the emperor, on his actions and character. So in Suetonius military campaigns and warfare, the staple subject matter of ancient historiography from Herodotos and Thucydides onwards, are not dealt with except where they reveal something about the emperor himself or his personal role. Another feature which is strikingly different from what we find in standard historiography is the lack of concern for chronology; indeed the bulk of most Suetonian Lives are not narrative at all. Take the biography of the 'Deified Augustus'. After a few pages on Augustus' ancestors, his birth and his boyhood – all standard elements in ancient biography – we find the following telescoped narrative of Augustus' rise to power and subsequent reign, all condensed into a few sentences:

> When Augustus first learned that Julius Caesar had been killed and he himself was his heir, he hesitated for some time as to whether he should appeal to the nearest legions, but eventually dismissed the idea as premature and hasty. Instead he returned to Rome and took up his inheritance, despite the doubts of his mother and the strong opposition of his stepfather, the ex-consul Marcius Philippus [44 BC]. Then he levied armies and from that time on held control of the state, first with M. Antony and M. Lepidus, and then just with Antony, for nearly twelve years [43-31 BC], and finally on his own for forty-four years [31 BC - AD 14].
>
> Having given, as it were, a summary of his life, I shall now set out the details one by one, not in chronological order but by topic, so that they can be explained and understood more clearly.
>
> (*Deified Augustus* 8-9)

The final sentence of this quotation is famous as a statement of method: the rest of the Life will not be chronological narrative, but will be organised thematically ('by topic'). Indeed, as we read on we are treated to a series of discussions of Augustus' habits and personal qualities, presented often without reference to chronology and grouped by theme.

Many are illustrated by anecdotes and examples. This abandoning of narrative marks a decisive break with the historical tradition. In Suetonius the spotlight is firmly on the palace and its intrigues, on the personal life of the emperor, his relations with his family, his dress, his sexual predilections and other such matters rather than on the traditional material of politics and war with which history typically concerned itself.

Some of Suetonius' biographies give a distinctly negative picture of the emperor, and have led many scholars to condemn Suetonius as a mere purveyor of cheap scandal and salacious gossip. But that would be a grave mistake. The themes on which Suetonius focuses and the details which he picks out are carefully chosen. Each emperor is measured up against a series of standards. The effect is to present an *assessment* or judgement of his qualities as ruler: was he a good emperor or a bad one, did he respect the Senate and the other members of the upper classes or not? The effect of the collection as a whole is to create a blue-print for what a good emperor should – and should not – be like. Take the following passage from the *Life of Nero*:

Gradually, however, as his vices grew stronger, he dropped jokes and subterfuge and with no attempt at concealment openly broke out into even more serious crimes.

He used to draw out his banquets from noon to midnight, reviving himself with warm baths or, in summer, with ice-cold ones. Sometimes he would even dine in public in the Campus Martius, where he would drain the artificial lake, or in the Circus Maximus, with the whole city's prostitutes and dancing girls as his retinue. Whenever he drifted down the Tiber to Ostia or cruised around the Bay of Baiae, guest houses were set out and made ready on the shores and banks along the way. These places were remarkable for their debauchery and their trade in respectable ladies, who would imitate tavern women and would solicit him from this side and that to call for them. He also used to force his friends to invite him for dinner. One of them spent four million sesterces on a party where people wore turbans, while another spent even more on a party accompanied by roses.

Besides seducing free-born boys and sleeping with married women, he also raped the Vestal Virgin Rubiria. He very nearly made the freed slave Acte his lawful wife, by bribing some men of consular rank to swear falsely that she had royal blood in her veins.

(*Nero* 27-8.1)

Suetonius here presents Nero as committing a series of outrages to traditional sensitivities. He is a drunkard: he drinks all day, not limiting his feasting to the evening as he should. Republican benefactors and other emperors had equipped Rome with aqueducts, Nero pollutes them by swimming in them. He encourages the ruin of the Senate, who were obliged to spend fortunes on entertainment and to wear disgraceful eastern dress, with all its connotations of luxury, effeminacy and tyranny. He carries on in public with prostitutes, and debauches children and married women. Worse that this, he rapes a Vestal Virgin, on whose chastity the safety of the state depended. Nero is everything an emperor should not be; he outrages the members of the elite and endangers the state.

This, then, is not scandal-mongering, but a carefully constructed and extended attack, designed to demonstrate what a bad emperor Nero was. In fact, the nearest ancient parallel to this kind of extended attack is to be found in law-court speeches, where accusations along similar lines are commonplace. This is quite significant: there is no sense here of the reader being left to make up his or her mind. Rather, as in a prosecution speech, he or she is carefully guided to specific conclusions about each emperor. Some emperors emerge well, some badly. But Suetonius' *Lives of the Caesar*s should certainly not be thought of as objective descriptions – as they are often taken to be. One final thing should be noted. Although Suetonius condemns some emperors like Nero, there is never any hint of criticism of the imperial system itself. The question is rather whether a particular emperor was a good one or a bad one.

Suetonius' *Lives of the Caesars* were certainly influential. They were being imitated as late as the fourth century AD, the probable date of the so-called *Historia Augusta* ('Imperial history'), a collection of short biographies of emperors from Hadrian onwards, which are full of scandal and anecdote. It is not clear whether the *Historia Augusta* is the work of one author or several; equally unclear are the circumstances of its collection and its tone (is it entirely serious?). Certainly it is notoriously unreliable. But it will not detain us much here, for from the second century AD onwards it is again to the Greek world that we must look for the most exciting developments in historiography.

Chapter 11

Greek historians of the Roman imperial period

Plutarch

Mainland Greece had been annexed by Rome in 146 BC; the remaining Hellenistic kingdoms gradually fell, until, with the conquering of Cleopatra's Egypt in 31 BC, almost all of the Greek-speaking cities lay under Roman control. Although many city-states remained autonomous, Roman governors were appointed to oversee the provinces into which the Greek world was now divided. The days of independent foreign policy had passed: Greek cities and Greek kings no longer fielded armies; the *pax Romana*, the peace brought by Roman control, prevented that. But the Greek city-states continued functioning. And although independent military action was no longer possible, it would be a mistake to think of Roman conquest as marking any kind of end or 'decline' in Greek cultural, artistic or intellectual life. Indeed, the second century AD in many ways marks a high point in Greek prosperity and cultural production. Of particular interest to us is the fascination shown by Greeks of this period for their own past, up to and including the Classical period – that is, up to Alexander the Great and his immediate successors. This fascination with the Classical past has been interpreted in various ways. It might be seen as a mark of renewed cultural self-confidence. Alternatively it might reveal a dissatisfaction with the peaceful and prosperous but rather circumscribed present under Roman rule, a hankering in other words after past glories.

Foremost in this historical movement was **Plutarch** (*c.* AD 45-120), who lived and worked in the small Boiotian town of Chaironeia. The range of Plutarch's literary output is staggering. He was a philosopher above all, but he had a strong interest in history too; and history he conceived in biographical terms. In the final decade of the first century AD (that is, just before Suetonius) he had already produced his own series of *Lives of the Caesars*, spanning from Augustus to Vitellius (AD 69). These are now unfortunately all lost, except for the short Lives of Galba and Otho. But Plutarch's larger collection, the *Parallel Lives*, written between about AD 100 and 120, survives almost in full.

The most striking and unique feature of the *Parallel Lives* is their

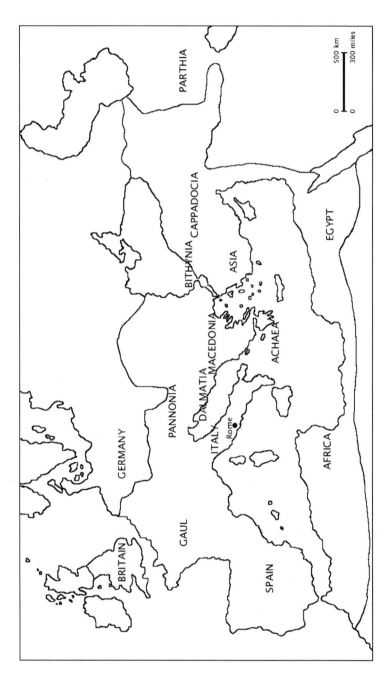

Fig. 6 The Roman Empire, c. AD 120

structure. Each of the twenty-two surviving books contains a biography of a Greek statesman or general paired with that of a Roman (usually but not always in that order): for example, Alexander the Great and Julius Caesar. The two biographies are often welded together with a short closing comparison, or *synkrisis*, which contrasts and compares the two men. (Unfortunately, this unique structure is not reflected in the most popular modern translations, which rip paired Lives apart and ignore the *synkrisis*.) The subject matter is the distant past and together the *Parallel Lives* cover a vast time-span. The Greek Lives cover the period from Theseus, mythical founder of Athens, to the Hellenistic kings, though most are concentrated in the Classical period. The Roman Lives run from Romulus, founder of Rome – who is paired for obvious reasons with Theseus – through the Republic to Mark Antony. In his biographical focus and his choice of which heroes to treat Plutarch was probably influenced by Nepos (see above, pp. 76-8). But the *Parallel Lives*, which run to between about 20 and 90 pages each in modern editions, are on an altogether different scale from the latter's brief biographies.

The aims and the scope of the *Parallel Lives* can perhaps best be gauged from the opening 'programmatic' words of the *Lives of Alexander and Caesar*:

> I am beginning in this book to write the life of Alexander the King and the life of that Caesar by whom Pompey was overthrown. But because of the great number of deeds which they carried out, I shall make no other preface than to beg my readers not to quibble if I do not report all of their famous achievements and do not give an exhaustive account of any of them, but summarise them for the most part. For it is not so much histories that I am writing but Lives, and the most outstanding deeds do not always reveal virtue or vice. But often a little matter like a saying or a joke hints at character more than battles where thousands die, huge troop deployments or the sieges of cities. So, just as painters aim to capture their subject's likeness from his face and the appearance of his eyes – by which character is hinted at – and pay very little attention to the other parts of the body, so I must be allowed to penetrate rather the signs of the soul, and through these to give shape to each man's life. I will accordingly leave to other writers a narrative of their great deeds and battles.   (*Life of Alexander* 1)

Several things are striking here. The first is the plea to the reader not to expect large-scale political and military narrative: the standard stuff of history. For Plutarch, what is central is the exploration of *character*. Thus, he claims, he will often prefer to select anecdotes and details of the subject's 'off-duty' moments, where they are particularly revealing of character, than simply to narrate his great exploits on the grand stage of politics and war. We have already noted something of this tendency to concentrate on character in the biographies of Suetonius. But whereas Suetonius' Lives are concerned simply with passing judgement on their subjects, in Plutarch's programme an understanding of the character of Alexander or of any other subject is meant to have a practical aim: to encourage introspection in the reader with the ultimate goal of his or her *moral improvement*. Indeed, it was the morally improving nature of Plutarch that made his *Parallel Lives* until about the middle of the nineteenth century by far the most widely read and loved of all works to survive from antiquity.

Plutarch's *Parallel Lives* are remarkable, then, both for their focus on the person of the individual subject and for their concern with issues of character and personal morality. A good example of this is provided by the *Lives of Perikles and Fabius Maximus*. Plutarch begins this pair of Lives by musing on the moral value of reading about virtuous men: when we read about the great men of the past, he says, we are inspired to copy or 'imitate' them and therefore to become better people ourselves. He continues:

> So we too have decided to persevere in our writing of their lives, and we have composed this book, the tenth in the series. It contains the life of Perikles and that of Fabius Maximus, who fought it out with Hannibal. They were men alike in their virtues in general, and especially in their calmness and justice and in their ability to bear the senseless attacks of their peoples and of their colleagues in office. They thus become most useful to their countries. But whether we aim correctly at what we should, can be decided from what we have written. (*Life of Perikles* 2.5)

Here Plutarch picks out explicitly the qualities or virtues which Perikles and Fabius had in common, in particular their calmness or steadfastness, that is, the ability to stick to their plans despite attacks and accusations from those around them. The reader is thus alerted early on to one of the main moral themes of the two Lives, and one of the key virtues which he or she might imitate. Indeed, as one reads on in the two Lives the calmness and rationality of Perikles and Fabius, in contrast to the passions of the mob and of their jealous rivals, are repeatedly highlighted and provide not only a moral focus but also a unifying literary force – something which binds the two Lives together into a single whole.

Of course, much of Plutarch's material for the *Life of Perikles* came directly from Thucydides. Indeed, for most of the figures whose biographies Plutarch writes there were available both to him and to his readers the works of earlier historians and other authors. Some of them, like Thucydides, were well-known classics. Plutarch himself is quite open about his debt to the literary tradition; indeed he often expects his reader to recognise the original passages and contexts on which he is drawing and which he often subtly alters or recasts. His Lives should not, then, be read so much as attempts at primary research, to inform the reader about periods or people about whom they had no knowledge (though, in fact, for us they often perform this function). Rather they are elegant compositions, which aim to represent well-known periods and personages in new ways which would be both interesting and morally edifying to Plutarch's readers.

A good example of various aspects of Plutarch's technique can be seen from his treatment of the childhood of Alexander the Great. It is at the start of the *Life of Alexander*, as we have seen, that Plutarch declares his concern with the subject's character and his practice of using the revealing anecdote in order to explore it (see above, pp. 109-10). Plutarch does just that in his story of the young Alexander taming the horse which was to become his trusted mount in so many battles, Boukephalas. Plutarch gives us a self-contained dramatic scene (*Alex.* 6). The king's attendants cannot break the horse in; Alexander makes a bet with his incredulous father that he can do it; he turns the horse towards the sun, as he has noticed that it was its own shadow which disturbed it, leaps on its back and successfully controls it. All are amazed. The scene ends with Alexander's father declaring, 'My son, seek out a kingdom which is your equal: Macedonia cannot hold you.' This provides the punch-line, as it were, to the passage, and suggests to the reader how it should be understood: Alexander was to conquer a huge kingdom abroad just as, and by the same courage, confidence and ambition, he had conquered Boukephalas. Indeed this confidence and ambition are central to Plutarch's portrait of Alexander. His Alexander the Great – like his Julius Caesar, with whom Alexander is paired – emerges as a man driven by ambition to great achievements, but whose ambition and inability to stop, combined with the power and success which these qualities bring, will finally lead him into superstition, megalomania and an early and tragic death. The *Lives of Alexander and Caesar* might, then, be read as a tragic lesson about the benefits and dangers of ambition; the story of the taming of Boukephalas signals this theme at the very start of the pair.

Plutarch goes on in this passage to discuss Alexander's own education and in doing so drops into the discussion a quotation from a play of Sophokles. This is a good reminder of how literary Plutarch's Lives are. So often the reader is challenged to spot and understand the numerous allusions which are made to earlier literature, including Plato, tragedy and the historians: Plutarch's *Parallel Lives* are above all works of literature, sophisticated and allusive. Their value to us as historical sources depends in part on the quality of the sources which Plutarch had at his disposal for any given Life, and also on the extent of survival of these and other sources to our own time. For the fifth-century Athenian Lives, for example, where some of Plutarch's most important sources survive (Herodotos, Thucydides, Xenophon), their historical value is limited. For other periods, such as those that dealt with Marius and Sulla, or with the Hellenistic kings Pyrrhos and Demetrios, Plutarch's Lives are much more valuable to the modern historian. But we should never lose sight of their avowed concern with character, which often leads Plutarch to prefer anecdote and allusion to the kind of detailed chronological narrative which a historian might like.

It has become fashionable, for the reasons outlined above, to reject Plutarch as a second-rate source. The injustice of this will be immediately apparent: Plutarch's first priority was not primary research but rather the presentation of the past in morally uplifting or challenging ways. It is worth noting in addition that Plutarch was not alone in his moral concerns. As we have seen, all ancient writers believed that history should in some sense be useful, and should have some kind of moral content, and all made choices and selections of what to include and what to leave out. Indeed, it is these choices and the assumptions which they reveal that can often be most illuminating; they shed light on the thought-world of the author and his society as much as on the periods about which he is writing. Thus, Plutarch's concentration in his Greek Lives on the period up to and including Alexander the Great – that is 400 years of so before he was writing – and his eschewal of more contemporary history, is most instructive. It tells us something about the growing sense which Greeks of this period had that Greek history stopped long ago; that the glories of Greece were long past. Furthermore, Plutarch's decision to construct his history around the pairing of Greek and Roman figures is itself interesting. Does it express an assumption of, or an attempt to demonstrate, the equality of Greek culture with Roman?

Arrian

This fascination with the Classical past can be seen very clearly in the work of another Greek historian, L. Flavius Arrianus (*c.* AD 86-160). **Arrian** belonged to the generation after Plutarch but, unlike Plutarch, pursued an outstanding career in the Roman administration, attained the consulship in AD 129 or 130 and even governed Cappadocia in Asia Minor, an important militarised province. His career is testimony to the fact that some members at least of the Greek elite were by this time able to reach the upper echelons of the Roman administrative machinery. These experiences certainly seem to have influenced Arrian's literary output. We hear, amongst various other lost texts, of a history of Rome's relations and wars with Parthia (the *Parthika*); he also wrote two works on the Alani, a tribe against which he himself saw action, one of which survives. But his most famous work, which survives in full, is a history in seven books of the conquests of Alexander the Great. The title by which this work was known, the *Anabasis* ('Journey Inland') *of Alexander*, recalls Xenophon's *Anabasis*, also in seven books (see above, pp. 39-40). It is no coincidence that it is to an Athenian author of the Classical period that Arrian looks for his model.

Alexander the Great was a popular figure for historians. We have already seen how Plutarch, at the start of his *Life of Alexander*, declares that he will concentrate on the little details that reveal character at the expense of a military narrative. Arrians's *Anabasis* is very different. It concentrates almost entirely on Alexander's military campaigns. There is nothing on Alexander's childhood or early years, none of the revealing vignettes of Alexander's private life, and none of the darker side, the sense of Alexander's growing megalomania, that we find in Plutarch. The opening words stress his choice of good sources:

Whenever Ptolemy son of Lagos and Aristoboulos son of Aristoboulos have both given the same accounts of Alexander son of Philip, I record what they say as completely true. But when they differ, I have chosen the version which seems to me more trustworthy and also more worth narrating. In fact, other writers have given a variety of accounts of Alexander; indeed there is no one else who has given rise to more historians or about whom there is less agreement. But in my view Ptolemy and Aristoboulos are the most trustworthy in their narrative … Anyone who is surprised that, in the face of so many other historians, it should have occurred to me to compose this history should restrain his surprise until he has first read all their works and then encountered my own.   (*Anabasis*, Preface)

As we noted earlier (p. 51), Aristoboulos and Ptolemy, who had accompanied Alexander on his campaigns, were the writers of 'authorised' accounts of Alexander's conquests, accounts which portrayed Alexander as a conquering hero and model king. Their work, lost to us, of course represented only one of the types of Alexander-histories that were being produced in the century or so following his death. There was also, as we have noted, the sensationalist, 'vulgate' tradition, and a hostile tradition. The hostile tradition certainly left its mark in places in Plutarch's *Life of Alexander*, and profoundly influenced the Roman writer Curtius Rufus, whose ten-book *History of Alexander*, written some time in the first two centuries AD, presents Alexander as degenerating into a drunk, irascible tyrant. Arrian's work shows no trace of this hostile tradition, but is instead almost without exception favourable to Alexander.

Arrian's Alexander, then, is an idealised figure, the quintessential king and general. Here, chosen almost at random, is a section from Book 3. Alexander is deep in Asia in hot pursuit of the Persian King Darius and his subordinate Bessus, who it seems has overthrown and arrested his master:

> On hearing this, Alexander decided that he must pursue with all his strength. Already his men and horses were becoming exhausted under the continued hardship. But he pressed on all the same, and covered a great deal of ground during the night and the following day until at noon he reached a village where Darius' captors had camped the previous day. As he heard there that the barbarians had taken the decision to travel by night, he began questioning the locals as to whether they knew of any short-cut to get to the fugitives. They replied that they did, but that the road was inhospitable through lack of water. He told them to guide him along this road, and since he realised that his infantry would not keep up with him if he pushed on at full speed, he dismounted about five hundred horsemen. He also selected from the officers of the infantry and of the other troops those who were performing best, and ordered them to mount their horses, with their usual infantry arms ... Alexander then started off himself at evening and led his troops on at a fast pace. During the night he covered up to four hundred stades [*c.* 50 miles] and as dawn was breaking he came upon the Persians who were proceeding in disorder and without arms ...   (*Anabasis* 3.21.6-9)

The impression is one of relentless action. Alexander is at the centre of events, directing and leading from the front. One might compare the picture which Caesar gives of himself in his *On the Gallic War* – a work

also influenced by Xenophon's *Anabasis* (see above, pp. 74-6). It is
Alexander himself, for example, rather than his subordinates or interpret-
ers, who discusses the route with the locals. This is representative of the
Anabasis as a whole, which is to a remarkable extent centred on the person
of Alexander. Throughout we see Alexander not only achieving great
exploits – here covering great distances quickly – but looking after and
caring for his men. He is, in other words, the ideal king and general. The
details of his dismounting some of his cavalry and giving their horses to
carefully picked officers drawn from the infantry are characteristic of
Arrian, whose account is full of such military technicalities. The recording
of such details makes Arrian an extremely valuable source for the history
of Alexander. But it need hardly be stressed that Arrian's work as a whole
is one-sided and far from neutral; there is nothing, for example, on
Alexander's conquests from the Persian point of view. It is almost relent-
lessly positive to Alexander; Arrian's sources, as we have also seen, were
Alexander's own generals. This is an excellent and valuable account, but
hardly an objective assessment.

As we have already noted, there were plainly in circulation when Arrian
was writing various stories of Alexander's brutality and increasingly
autocratic behaviour. Plutarch dealt with this tradition by painting a
picture of Alexander's gradual moral decline and corruption as his power
increased. Arrian, on the other hand, largely ignores such stories. There is
just one point in the work where Arrian gives any attention to this negative
material. In the middle of Book 4, and in fact near the mid-point of the
work as a whole, Arrian gathers together and discusses – out of chronological sequence – a number of the most well-known of these potentially
damaging stories (4.7-14). The section begins with Alexander's mutilation of Bessus, the Persian who had overthrown and later murdered Darius,
and continues to discuss more general accusations that Alexander had
gradually adopted eastern clothes and manners:

I myself do not praise this extreme punishment of Bessus, but count
the mutilation of extremities as barbaric. I agree that Alexander was
carried away into imitation of Persian and Median wealth and of the
habit prevalent among the barbarians by which their kings do not
live on equal terms with their subjects. I do not praise the fact that
though a descendant of Herakles he exchanged Persian clothes for
his Macedonian ancestral ones and that he was not ashamed to
exchange the tiara of the Persians whom he had defeated for the
garments that he himself, their victor, had long worn.

I do not praise any of these things, but I take Alexander's great successes as clearer proof than anything else that neither strength of body, nor noble birth nor continuous good fortune in war greater even than Alexander's – not even if one could sail round Libya and Asia and gain possession of both of them, just as Alexander in fact intended, not even if one added Europe to Asia and Libya – none of these things contributes to a man's happiness unless the man who has apparently achieved such great things can at the same time control himself.

At this point it will not be out of place to record what happened to Kleitos and the suffering of Alexander on his account, even though it was actually done a little later.   (4.7.4-8.1)

Arrian goes on to describe Alexander's murder in a drunken rage of his friend Kleitos. He concludes by criticising Alexander for anger and drunkenness, but also throwing some of the blame on Kleitos for aggravating Alexander and commending Alexander for showing remorse afterwards. Although plainly here Arrian does criticise Alexander, the overall effect of gathering all these accusations together and getting them out of the way quickly, and of commending Alexander's remorse for his wrongdoings, seems to be to minimise the effect of such damaging material.

One can only speculate as to what connection there might be between this idealised presentation of Alexander the Great and the context in which works like Arrian's were being produced. Certainly Roman emperors like Trajan were being frequently compared to Alexander, and often as not encouraged the comparison. Trajan had indeed in AD 114-116 fought a series of wars against Parthia, which the propaganda of the time presented as the successor to the Persian Empire. An account like Arrian's, then, might well be read as glorifying the Roman emperor, while at the same time implicitly providing a model for how emperors should and should not behave. It is also possible that a work like Arrian's reflects deeper cultural anxieties. In a world in which military power now lay firmly with Rome, the *Anabasis* could be read as an expression of longing for a lost and distant past; but Arrian's conquering Alexander could equally be read as a symbol of Greek military power, the *Anabasis* as an assertion that the Greeks could boast a conqueror and an empire to rival any other.

Appian

Not all Greek historians were looking away from Rome to the glories that were Greece. The two historians with whom we shall close both dealt directly with Rome, though from rather different perspectives. At roughly the same time as Arrian was working, the Egyptian-Greek historian **Appian** (*c.* AD 95-160s) was composing his *Roman History* (*Romaika*). Appian's work is an attempt to interpret and explain Roman history to a Greek readership – especially the history of her expansion. A major literary influence must have been Polybios (see above, pp. 56-60). But Appian's work is a good deal shorter than Polybios' (24 books, of which Books 6-9 and 11-17 survive in full), and the arrangement rather different. In particular the structure is *geographical*. Different books or groups of books deal with Rome's involvement with and conquest of different geographical areas or peoples. The last books (18-24), now lost, dealt in apparently great depth with the annexation of Egypt, Appian's own country, and then took the story up to Trajan and his conquests. For this emphasis on his own homeland we might compare the work of the Jewish historian Josephus (born *c.* AD 37) whose works the *Jewish War* and *Jewish Antiquities*, both written in Greek, trace the history of the Jews from earliest times to his own period. But for Appian, Roman activity is always centre-stage. He claimed indeed in his preface that his last book would 'show the present military force of the Romans, the income they enjoy from each nation, what they spend on naval defence and other such things' (Preface 15).

Appian is an extremely important source for Roman history. His account of the civil wars in Books 13-17 is the only unbroken narrative by any writer, Greek or Roman, to survive of this important period. (These books are often referred to by modern historians under the title *Civil Wars*, though it has to be remembered that this is merely a section of the wider whole.) Appian plainly made use of the work of many earlier authors now lost to us, such as Asinius Pollio (see above, p. 85) and the sections of Polybios which have not survived. There has been accordingly a tendency to regard his work merely as the vehicle by which information from these earlier writers has been preserved. But we should not lose sight of what is distinctive about his work: this is Roman history written from a Greek, provincial perspective (cf. the remarks on Diodoros, above, p. 50).

This provincial perspective is apparent right from the preface to the work as a whole, where, after summarising the extent of the Roman Empire, Appian declares:

> Because I thought that someone else might want to learn about the Romans in this way, I am writing about each nation separately. I omit whatever happened to others in the meantime and transfer these to their proper place. I have considered it superfluous to put down the dates for everything, but I shall mention here and there the dates for the most outstanding events.   (Preface 13)

This is history from the outside in. It is no surprise that Appian goes on in this paragraph to offer an explanation of the Roman system of names (*praenomen, nomen* and *cognomen*) something which Plutarch also felt obliged to explain (e.g. *Coriolanus* 11; *Marius* 1) and which might have confused his Greek readers; both Plutarch and Appian often take care to explain unfamiliar Latin words or aspects of Roman culture. The organisation along ethnic and geographic lines is itself significant: the spotlight is successively thrown on the different peoples that were conquered by Rome and incorporated in the Empire. This is very different from the accounts of Livy, Tacitus or Suetonius, in which the Senate and the city of Rome itself remain centre-stage. For example, in the section which deals with the Roman civil wars Appian shows a much greater interest than any Roman writer in the position of the Italian peoples of Italy – at that time not Roman citizens but bound to fight for Rome in her armies and often exploited. Appian is also unique in the attention he gives to the Roman equestrians – the non-Senatorial nobility – and the influence that they had on Roman policy. Appian's own origins in Egypt can perhaps be seen in his insistence that the conquest of Egypt was the culmination and high point of Roman expansion – though unfortunately, as mentioned earlier, the books that dealt with this are now lost. But particularly notable is his acceptance of the fact and necessity of monarchy, which is presented as saving Rome from a cycle of violence: contrast Tacitus' bitter critique of its failings. Once again, Appian probably reflects the views of his educated provincial readership, for whom the story of how Rome became a monarchy and how its provinces were gradually incorporated into its growing empire might well have been interesting, but the fact of monarchic rule itself was probably not controversial.

Cassius Dio

We finish our survey of the historians of Greece and Rome by moving a century later. **Cassius Dio** (born *c.* AD 164) was a Greek from Bithynia in Asia Minor. But like Arrian several generations earlier, he pursued a successful career in the Roman administration. He was twice consul, and served in the 220s successively as governor of Africa, Dalmatia and Upper Pannonia (the latter two important military posts). The early third century AD was a turbulent one. The stability of the Roman Empire, which earlier historians had taken for granted, was under serious threat. Foreign invasions, palace coups and numerous civil wars proliferate. The ruling classes had to learn to cope with a succession of violent and unpredictable emperors. In the context of these difficult times, Dio wrote in Greek a

Roman History, which dealt in a mammoth 80 books with the history of Rome from its foundations until the date of his own consulship in AD 229. Only the section from 69-6 BC (roughly Books 36-55) survives in full, though we may get some idea of the lost books from the quotations and summaries which survive in the works of later writers.

Dio's history brings together many of the themes which we have noticed. First, it is annalistic – that is, it is structured year by year, each year beginning with the names of the consuls and any notable omens or portents. It is striking that Dio, a Greek, should adopt this quintessentially Roman literary form – but this shows us how meaningless simplistic distinctions between Greek and Roman may be for the wealthy men of the eastern part of the empire in this period. But overlaying this annalistic framework there is also a biographical organisation: the work is structured around the lives of great individuals and, for imperial times, according to the reigns of successive emperors. We have already noted the increasing tendency under Roman emperors to see history in biographical terms – for obvious reasons (see above, p. 104).

Dio certainly saw himself as writing within a long historiographical tradition. His Greek is rather archaising, and seems to have been modelled on that of Thucydides. But he is also very contemporary. In his analysis of Roman history he raises issues which were of concern to his own elite readers. As we have remarked so often in this book, a historian often reveals as much about his own age and its concerns as about the age of which he is writing. Perhaps the best examples of the contemporary relevance of Dio's work can be seen in the so-called Constitutional Debate in Book 52. The scene is set in 29 BC, and two courtiers of Augustus discuss the best constitution for Augustus to impose on Rome: should the Republic be restored, or is a monarchy the best solution, the proposal that actually wins the day? The model for this is plainly Herodotos' Constitutional Debate in Book 3 of his *Histories* (see above, p. 20). But the debate allows Dio to explore issues of contemporary relevance. In particular the details of what sort of monarchy is proposed can easily be read as a comprehensive analysis of the kind of reforms necessary to the current system of imperial government in Dio's own day. As so often the past is used to comment on and explore issues of contemporary significance.

500	Birth of Athenian democracy (508)	
	Battle of Marathon (490)	
	Xerxes' invasion of Greece (480)	
		Hekataios
		Herodotos
	Peloponnesian War (431-404)	
		Thucydides
		Hellanikos
400		
	Gallic Sack of Rome (390)	'Oxyrhynchos historian'
	King's Peace (386)	Xenophon
		Ephoros
		Theopompos
	Philip defeats Greek states (338)	
	Death of Alexander (323)	Kallisthenes
		Aristoboulos and Ptolemy
300		
		Timaios
		Douris of Samos
		Phylarchos
	First Punic War (264-241)	
	Second Punic War (218-201)	
		Naevius
200		*Ennius*
		Fabius Pictor
		Cato the Elder
	Battle of Pydna (168)	
	Sack of Carthage;	
	annexation of Greece (146)	Polybios
	Jugurthine War (112-105)	
100		
	Dictatorship of Sulla (82-80)	
		Diodoros

Caesar in Gaul (58-49)
Assassination of Julius Caesar (44) *Sallust*
Battle of Actium (31 BC) *Nepos, Asinius Pollio*
Nikolaos of Damascus
Dionysios of Halikarnassos
Livy

Accession of Tiberius (AD 14)

Velleius Paterculus

Year of Four Emperors (AD 68-69)

Curtius Rufus
Josephus

Accession of Nerva (AD 96)
100

Plutarch
Tacitus
Suetonius
Arrian
Appian

Civil war (AD 193)
200

Cassius Dio

Fig. 7 Chronological table showing historians and major events. The names of historians who wrote in Latin are printed in italics. Note that historians are placed roughly according to the period at which they wrote, not according to their dates of birth or death. Given that many worked over a period of several decades, and many were contemporaneous with each other, this table is approximate only. Note also that most of the fragmentary historians have been omitted.

Epilogue

We finish our survey of the Greek and Roman historians with Cassius Dio. The third century AD in many ways marks an important change. The Roman Empire entered a period of crisis of massive proportions, and began to break into two. The safety of the provinces or of Rome itself could no longer be guaranteed. Constantinople and the Greek-speaking part of the Empire became increasingly distant from Rome and the West as both parts fought for their survival. Over the next five hundred years or so the vast majority of authors and texts were lost; what survived was a mere fraction of the treasures of ancient literature that crumbled as manuscripts decayed through neglect or were burnt. But those few classics that were preserved began in the Middle Ages to be read and imitated again, both in the Latin-speaking West and especially in the Byzantine East. And from the Renaissance onwards, when there was a rediscovery of ancient literature, the Greek and Roman historians exerted a tremendous influence on the development of modern historiography. They bequeathed to more recent generations not only a fascinating and vivid picture of the worlds of Greece and Rome, albeit distorted and fragmented, but also a sense of what writing history was about.

As we have stressed throughout this book, the ancient historians saw themselves as writing in a literary tradition stretching back unbroken to Herodotos and Thucydides, and ultimately to Homer; they constructed their narratives carefully, sometimes with moral or political lessons in mind for their readers. Many cared deeply about their sources and their accuracy. But most believed too that the historian himself played a vital creative role: he had the responsibility to give shape and meaning to the events, periods or lives he recounted. The best ancient authors did not often make the mistake – and nor should we – of believing that they were simply writing down 'what really happened'.

Suggestions for further study

1. Introduction

In what ways did Homer's *Iliad* provide a model for future historians? Does the *Iliad* still exert any influence on the way history is written today? Does history always have heroes?

2. Herodotos

Herodotos suggested that it is possible to discern the hand of God in history. Do you believe this? What would his readers have made of his presentation of the Persian Wars as a tale of arrogance punished and virtue winning through? Herodotos wrote at the height of Athens' imperial power. Might his readers have seen any contemporary warning? Why did Herodotos spend so much time writing about the customs of other peoples? What do you think of his policy of 'saying what is being said' (p. 17)?

3. Thucydides

What was Thucydides' contribution to the practice of history? Is it right to see him as an objective historian? Are there any themes or events which Thucydides does not cover and which we would like to know more about? Would it be plausible to regard Thucydides as a 'tragic historian' (see pp. 53-6). So much of what we know of the political and military events of the fifth century is derived from Thucydides. Can you imagine what our picture of this period would be like if Thucydides' work had not survived?

4. Fourth-century historians

How does Xenophon's *Hellenika* differ from Thucydides' work? Does it make any difference to know that Xenophon also wrote a philosophical work about Sokrates and a praise-speech (*enkomion*) about Agesilaos? In dealing with lost authors, in what sense might the term 'fragment' be misleading? What are the dangers of trying to reconstruct the approaches of lost historians from their fragments? Are there any problems with using Diodoros to reconstruct Ephoros and the Oxyrhynchos historian?

5. Hellenistic historians

Some historians attacked their rivals for a 'tragic' style. What did they mean by this? Should we take these attacks at face value? Is a 'tragic' style always a bad thing? Do modern historians ever use it? What effects did the conquests of Alexander the Great have on the practice of history? How did Greek writers deal with the coming of the Romans?

6. Roman Republican historians

How did early Roman historians differ from their Greek contemporaries? Were they influenced by Greek models? Was Sallust addressing any wider themes in writing about Catiline and Jugurtha? Does it make any difference that Cicero saw the historian's task as akin to that of the orator? Is Caesar's *On the Gallic War* history or propaganda? Can you always distinguish the two? Who do you think was the intended audience for Nepos' *Lives of Illustrious Men*?

7. Livy

Would Augustus have been happy with Livy's history? What was there in Livy's account which might have attracted his readers? Livy claims in his preface that his history will be 'useful' to his readers. Do you think this was really the case? Is studying history ever useful?

8. Imperial Rome

What problems did the imperial system present to the historian? Why is it important to know the social, cultural or geographical background of the historian?

9. Historians of imperial Rome: Tacitus

Are there any factors which might make us question whether Tacitus really gives us a reliable picture of the first century AD? Was Tiberius a bad emperor? Robert Graves famously used Tacitus' *Annals* as the basis for his historical novels *I Claudius* and *Claudius the God*. Are there any similarities between Tacitus, or other ancient historians, and the modern historical novel? What does that show us about ancient historiography?

9. Historians of imperial Rome: other voices

How does Suetonius' approach differ from that of Tacitus? Suetonius gives us many fascinating details about the lives of individual emperors, but can we learn anything from his biographies about the imperial system as a whole or the way in which it was regarded? What would the Emperor Hadrian have made of Suetonius' *Lives of the Caesars*? Should we dismiss

Velleius Paterculus as a mere 'spin-doctor' for the regime? Does his account have any value for the modern historian?

10. Greek historians of the Roman imperial period
What did Greek historians of this period write about? What explanations have been offered for this? Why is it important to read Plutarch's *Parallel Lives* in the pairs in which they were written? What was his purpose in writing? How different is this from the purposes of, say, Thucydides, Livy or Tacitus? Is Plutarch a reliable source? Does Arrian give an objective account of Alexander the Great? How do you think Appian might have presented Egypt and its conquest by the Romans? Cassius Dio's style is plainly influenced by Thucydides, and his Constitutional Debate in Book 52 by Herodotos, both of whom wrote some six and a half centuries earlier. What does this show about the way in which ancient historians conceived their task?

How different are the ways in which the ancient Romans and Greeks wrote history to the ways in which it is done in the modern world? Are modern approaches better? Is there anything we have lost? Which is more similar to an ancient work of history: a modern history textbook or a modern historical novel?

Suggestions for further reading

Texts
Many of the authors discussed in this book can be found in paperback translation from either *Penguin Classics* (Penguin Books: Harmondsworth) or *Oxford World Classics* (Oxford University Press); some have also been published by Hackett Publishing Compay Inc. (Indianapolis). The introductions to many of the more recent of volumes of all three series are excellent.

Penguin Classics
Appian, *The Civil Wars*
Arrian, *The Campaigns of Alexander*
Cassius Dio, *The Roman History: The Reign of Augustus* [Books 50-6]
Herodotus, *The Histories*
Julius Caesar, *The Civil War*
Julius Caear, *The Conquest of Gaul*
Homer, *The Iliad* [several editions by different translators]
Joesphus, *The Jewish War*
Livy, *Early History of Rome* [Books 1-5]
Livy, *Rome and Italy* [Books 6-10]
Livy, *War with Hannibal* [Books 21-30]
Livy, *Rome and the Mediterranean* [Books 31-45]
Plutarch, *The Rise and Fall of Athens* [various Greek Lives]
Plutarch, *The Age of Alexander* [various Greek Lives]
Plutarch, *The Makers of Rome* [various Roman Lives]
Plutarch, *The Fall of the Roman Republic* [various Roman Lives]
Polybios, *The Rise of the Roman Empire* [abridged translation]
Quintus Curtius Rufus, *The History of Alexander*
Sallust, *The Jugurthine War / The Conspiracy of Catiline*
Suetonius, *The Twelve Caesars*
Tacitus, *The Agricola / The Germania*
Tacitus, *The Annals of Imperial Rome*
Tacitus, *The Histories*
Thucydides, *History of the Peloponnesian War*

Xenophon, *A History of My Times* [The *Hellenika*]
Xenophon, *The Persian Expedition* [The *Anabasis*]

Oxford World Classics
Herodotos, *The Histories*
Homer, *The Iliad*
Julius Caesar, *The Civil War*
Julius Caesar, *The Gallic War*
Livy, *The Rise of Rome* [Books 1-5]
Livy, *The Dawn of the Roman Empire* [Books 31-40]
Plutarch, *Greek Lives* [various Greek lives]
Plutarch, *Roman Lives* [various Roman lives]
Suetonius, *Lives of the Caesars*
Tacitus, *Agricola and Germany*
Tacitus, *The Histories*

Hackett
Herodotus, *The War between East and West* [selections]
Homer, *The Iliad* [also *The Essential Iliad* and *The Essential Homer*: selections]
Thucydides, *The Peloponnesian War*
Tacitus, *Annals*

Less well-known authors have not yet made it into these collections (though they may be added in the future) and can be consulted in the bilingual editions of the *Loeb Classical Library* (Harvard University Press: Cambridge, Mass. and Heineman: London). These edititons, which have the original Latin or Greek text on one side of the page and English translation on the other, are recommended for those with some knowledge of the original language. They are also useful for reading Plutarch's *Parallel Lives* as they retain the paired structure, and print the closing *synkriseis* (see p. 109) – both of which are ignored by Penguin and Oxford World Classics.

The Oxyrhynchos Historian is available in English only in an edition by S.J. Kern and P.R. McKechnie entitled *Hellenica Oxyrrhyncha* (Warminster 1988). The fragments of the lost historians have not been translated; the definitive editions in Greek and Latin respectively are by F. Jacoby, *Die Fragmente der griechischen Historiker* (Berlin and Leiden 1923-58; Leiden 1994-) and H. Peter, *Historicorum Romanorum reliquiae* (Leipzig, reprinted 1993).

Introductions

Two good series exist: T.J. Luce, *The Greek Historians*, and R. Mellor, *The Roman Historians*, both from Routledge (London 1997 and 1999), and J.M. Marincola, *Greek Historians*, and C.K. Kraus and A.J. Woodman, *Latin Historians* (*Greece and Rome: New Surveys in the Classics* 31 [Oxford 2001] and 27 [Oxford 1997]). J.M. Marincola's *Authority and Tradition in Ancient Historiography* (Cambridge 1997) is also excellent. Good collections of recent articles can be found in S. Hornblower's *Greek Historiography* (Oxford 1994), and C.S. Kraus' *The Limits of Historiography* (Leiden 1999).

The debate over the reliability of the ancient historians – between those who stress the literary nature and moral content of such texts and those who emphasise their historical reliability – can best be appreciated by comparing A.J. Woodman's *Rhetoric in Classical Historiography* (London and Sydney 1988) with P.J. Rhodes' article 'In Defence of the Greek Historians' in *Greece and Rome* 41 (1994), pp. 156-71.

Herodotos

The best general introduction is J. Gould, *Herodotus* (New York 1989). On Herodotos' ethnographic sections as offering a mirror-image of Greek culture, see F. Hartog, *The Mirror of Herodotus* (Berkeley 1989).

Thucydides

Two introductory books are worth noting: J. Hornblower, *Thucydides* (Oxford 1987), and G. Cawkwell, *Thucydides and the Peloponnesian War* (London and New York 1997).

Fourth-century historians

A useful chapter on the continuators of Thucydides, and on other sources of evidence for fourth-century history, is to be found in P.A. Cartledge, *Agesilaos and the Crisis of Sparta* (London 1987), ch. 5. On Xenophon, see J. Dillery, *Xenophon and the History of his Times* (London and New York 1995), and V.J. Gray, *The Character of Xenophon's Hellenica* (London 1989). On Theopompos, see also G.S. Shrimpton, *Theopompus the Historian* (Montreal and London 1991) and M.A. Flower, *Theopompus of Chios* (Oxford 1994). See also P.A. Brunt's article, 'On Historical Fragments and Epitomes', in *Classical Quarterly* 30 (1980), pp. 477-94. See also on Diodoros, below.

Alexander historians

The best summary is in P.A. Brunt, introduction to the Loeb edition of *Arrian: History of Alexander and Indica*, vol. 1 (Cambridge, Mass. 1976), pp. xviii-xxxiv. See below on Arrian.

Hellenistic historians and 'tragic history'
F.W. Walbank's article 'History and Tragedy', *Historia* 9 (1960), pp. 216-34 (reprinted in his *Selected Papers* (Cambridge 1985), pp. 224-41.

Polybios
A good introduction is F.W. Walbank's *Polybius* (Berkeley, Los Angeles and London 1972). More complex is A.M. Eckstein, *Moral Vision in the Histories of Polybius* (Berkeley 1995).

Dionysios of Halikarnassos
A good starting point is C. Schultze's 'Dionysius of Halicarnassus and his Audience' in I.S. Moxon et al., *Past Perspectives: Studies in Greek and Roman Historical Writing*, pp. 121-41 (Cambridge 1986). See also E. Gabba's *Dionysius and the History of Archaic Rome* (Berkeley 1991) and M. Fox's article, 'History and Rhetoric in Dionysius of Halicarnassus', in *Journal of Roman Studies* 83 (1993), pp. 31-47.

Diodoros
Recent work along the lines suggested on p. 50 is being done by K. Sacks. See his *Diodorus Siculus and the First Century* (Princeton 1990) and his article, 'Diodorus and his Sources: Conformity and Creativity', in S. Hornblower's *Greek Historiography* (Oxford 1994), pp. 213-32.

Early Roman historians
See E. Badian's 'The Early Historians', in T.A. Dorey's *Latin Historians* (London 1966), pp. 1-38; S.P. Oakley, *A Commentary on Livy: Books VI-X. Vol. 1: Introduction and Book VI* (Oxford 1997), pp. 72-104.

Sallust
D.S. Levene, 'Sallust's *Jugurtha*: An "Historical Fragment"', in *Journal of Roman Studies* 82 (1992), pp. 53-70.

Caesar
See the recent collection edited by K. Welch and A. Powell, *Julius Caesar as Artful Reporter: The War Commentaries as Political Instruments* (Duckworth / Classical Press of Wales 1998).

Livy
A good starting point is P.G. Walsh's *Livy: His Historical Aims and Methods* (Cambridge 1961). See also the introduction to S.P. Oakley's *A Commentary on Livy: Books VI-X. Vol. 1: Introduction and Book VI*

(Oxford 1997). On the sack of Rome, try T.J. Luce, 'Design and Structure in Livy: 5.32-55', *Transactions of the American Philological Association* 102 (1971), pp. 265-302.

Tacitus
For introductions try F.R.D. Goodyear, *Tacitus* (*Greece and Rome New Surveys in the Classics* 4: Oxford 1970); R.H. Martin, *Tacitus* (London 1981); R. Mellor, *Tacitus* (New York and London 1993). R. Syme's two-volume *Tacitus* (Oxford 1958) also remains standard reading.

Velleius Paterculus
See A.J. Woodman 'Velleius Paterculus' in T. A. Dorey's, *Empire and Aftermath: Silver Latin II* (London and Boston 1975), pp. 1-25.

Suetonius
The best introduction is A. Wallace-Hadrill, *Suetonius: The Scholar and his Caesars* (London 1983; New Haven 1984). An excellent analysis of the *Life of Nero* is found in T.S. Barton's article 'The *inventio* of Nero: Suetonius', in J. Elsner and J. Masters (eds), *Reflections of Nero* (Chapel Hill and London 1994), pp. 48-63.

Plutarch
T.E. Duff, *Plutarch's Lives: Exploring Virtue and Vice* (Oxford 1999; paperback 2002). Many important papers are collected in B. Scardigli (ed.), *Essays on Plutarch's Lives* (Oxford 1995) and C.B.R. Pelling, *Plutarch and History: Eighteen Studies* (London 2002).

Arrian
P.A. Stadter, *Arrian of Nicomedia* (Chapel Hill 1980). A.B. Bosworth, *From Arrian to Alexander: Studies in Historical Interpretation* (Oxford 1988). See above on the earlier Alexander historians.

Appian and Cassius Dio
Appian is particularly badly served by modern studies. A.M. Gowing's *The Triumviral Narratives of Appian and Cassius Dio* (Ann Arbour 1992) provides an introduction to both authors. On Dio there is also F. Millar, *A Study of Dio Cassius* (Oxford 1964), and J.W. Rich (ed.), *Cassius Dio: The Augustan Settlement. Roman History 53-55.9* (Warminster 1991).

Index

ab urbe condita, 64, 79, 83
Achaian League, 56-7
Achilles, 11, 15
Actium, battle of, 66, 79, 84-5
Africa, 57, 63-7, 69-70, 118
Aischylos, 15, 23-4
Agamemnon, 11
Agesilaos, 40-2, 44-5
Agricola, 93-4, 100
Aineias Taktikos, 59
Alani, 113
Alesia, 75
Alexander the Great, 46-7, 51-2, 100
    historians of, 51-2, 61, 107-16
Alkibiades, 32-3, 50
Amphipolis, 25, 32
Anabasis, 39-40, 113-16
Anaximander, 16
anecdotes, anecdotal technique,
    19-20, 31, 104-6, 109-13
anger, 11, 44, 116
annalistic history, 63-4, 67, 71, 76-7,
    81, 94, 119
Annals, Pontifical, 63, 72
Antony, M., 66, 79, 85, 104, 109
apodeiktike historia, 59
Appian, 61, 92, **116-18**
aqueducts, 105-6
archaeology (literary term), 26-7,
    31-2
archaeology (modern discipline), 44,
    92
Archidamian War, 30 (*see also* Peace
    of Nikias)
Archidamos, 49
archives, 74 (*see also* Annals,
    Pontifical)
aristocratic families, Roman, 64-5,
    69-70, 82 (*see also* Senate)

Aristotle, 43, 60
Arrian, 51, 61, 92, **113-16**
Asinius Pollio, 85, 117
Aristoboulos, 51, 113-14
Artabanos, 22-4
Asia Minor, 13-15, 19, 39-40, 44-5,
    65
Athenian Empire, 25, 29, 32, 35-6,
    42 (*see also* Peloponnesian
    War, causes of)
Athens, 13, 22-43
    surrender of (404), 30, 39-40
Atticus, 76
Augustus (Octavian), 60, 66, 79-81,
    83, 85-6, 90-1, 96-7, 99, 104,
    107, 119
autocracy, *see* monarchy

barbarians, 15, 26
Bessus, 114-15
bias, of historians, 15, 29-33, 40-3,
    46, 56, 67-8, 71-2, 84, 91, 96-7
biography, biographical focus, 31,
    46-7, 51-2, 60, 76-8, 103-16,
    119
Black Sea, 39
Boiotia, Boiotian League, 42, 44-5
book divisions, 19
Boukephalas, 111
Britain, 65, 74-6, 93-4
Brutus, regicide and first consul, 87,
    96
Brutus, assassin of Caesar, 66, 90
Byzantines, 122

Caesar, Julius, 65-6, 69, **74-6**, 79,
    104, 109, 111, 114-15
Calgacus, 68, 94
Caligula, 90, 96

Camillus, 88-9
Carthage, 57-8, 63-5, 85, 102
Cassius (tyrannicide), 66, 90
Cassius Dio, 92, **118-19**, 122
Catiline, 66-8
Cato the Elder, 64-5
Cato the Younger, 66, 69
Catullus, 76
causes of wars, analysis of, 28-31, 59
chastity, *see* women
chronology, 31, 41, 45, 48-9, 58, 60,
        68, 72, 104, 112
Cicero, 15, 67-8, **71-4**, 76, 79, 85
city-state, decline of?, 51, 107
civil war, 35, 37-8, 65-71, 74-6, 78-9,
        84-5, 90, 94-5, 117-18 (*see
        also* Year of Four Emperors)
Classicism, 61, 107, 111-13, 116, 119
Claudius, 90, 96, 101
Cleopatra, 107
Cloelius Antipater, 67
closure, lack of, 41, 70-1
commemorative function of history,
        15, 17-18
comparison (literary technique), 69,
        77-8, 100, 107-12, 116
Constitutional Debate (in Herodotos),
        20, 34, 119
'construction', 20, 24, 29, 34, 36, 40,
        43, 72-5, 81, 86, 101, 106,
        112, 122
Constantinople, 122
consuls, 60, 63, 66, 69, 81, 83, 87,
        94, 96-7
continuation, one history of another,
        29, 39-41, 44, 46, 48, 55
Corfu, *see* Kerkyra
Corinth, 19, 25, 29, 34, 42, 57, 64-5,
        85
corruption, 66-70, 83-5
Cossus, A. Cornelius, 82-3
Crassus, M. Licinius, 83
Cremutius Cordus, 90-1
Croesus, 18-19, 23
cultural relativism, 15-16, 77-8
Curtius Rufus, 52, 114
Cyrus, pretender to Persian throne,
        39-40
Darius, 114-15

decades, hexads, pentads, 81, 88, 96
Delian league, *see* Athenian Empire
Delos, 50
Delphoi, 22
Demaratos, 20-1
Demetrios Poliorketes, 112
democracy, 13, 20, 32, 47, 60, 101
Dio Cassius, see Cassius Dio
Diodoros, 45-6, **49-50**, 60, 76
Dionysios of Halikarnassos, 48, **60-1**
Domitian, 90-1, 93-6, 100, 104
Douris of Samos, 55
dramatic and/or exciting presentation,
        12, 20-1, 34-7, 39-40, 46,
        52-6, 58-9, 71-4, 82, 86-9,
        94-5, 97-8, 100-11, 111 (*see
        also* 'tragic history')
dreams, 22-4

eclipses, 16, 63
economics, ignored by ancient
        historians, 12, 31-2
editions, *see* translations
Egypt, 18-20, 44, 51, 58, 65, 79,
        117-18
elaboration of material, 55-6, 71-5,
        101, 122
Emperors, difficulty of writing
        history under, 90-2, 96-8,
        103-4
enkomion (praise-speech), 40, 93-4
Ennius, 63
entertainment, a goal of the historian,
        37, 47, 52-6, 58, 86, 97-8 (*see
        also* dramatic and/or exciting
        presentation; vividness, an aim
        of the historian)
Epameinondas, 42
Ephoros, **48-9**, 55, 58
epic poetry
        Greek, *see* Homer
        Roman, 63
epigrams, 70, 95-6, 111
epitaphios, *see* funeral speech
equestrians, 91, 103, 118
Eretria, 13-14, 24
ethnography, *see* geography
Etruscans, 81-2
Euboia, 13, 28-9

Eurymedon, battle of, 77
examples, exemplars, 84-9, 95, 110
exile, historians in, 25, 46
eyewitnesses, 27-8, 31

Fabius Pictor, **63-4**
fiction, modern, 73, 124-5
Flavians, 80, 90
fortune, 58-60, 97
fragments, 39, 44, 46-7, 55, 127 (*see also* loss of most ancient historians)
Funeral Speech of Perikles, 34-5

Galba, 99-100, 102
Germany, 65, 93
gods, *see* religious dimension to history
Greek
    contemporary weakness?, 61, 107, 112-13, 116
    influences on Roman historians, 63, 67, 72-4, 76-8, 86
    language of early Roman historians, 64
Gyges, 19, 23

Hades, 11, 48
Hadrian, 103, 106
Halikarnassos, 13-16
Hannibal, 57, 64, 78, 81-2, 88
Hebrew Bible, 16
Hekataios, 16, 56, 93
Helen, 11, 17
Hellanikos of Lesbos, 61
Hellespont, 22, 51
Herakleitos, 16, 18
Herakles, 48, 115
Herodotos
    life and works, **13-24**, 28, 56
    influence of, 43, 46-8, 52, 84, 87-8, 93, 101, 104, 112, 122
hexads, *see* decades
Hippias, 24
*historia/historie,*15-16, 19-20
*Historia Augusta,*106
historian revealing about his own society, 50, 52, 78, 91, 112, 116-18 (*see also* 'mirror' of Herodotos)

history repeats itself, 37-8
Homer, influence of, 11-12, 15-18, 20-2, 26-8, 63, 120
hybris, 21-4, 35-6

ideal king, emperor or general, 51, 75-6, 94, 102, 105-6, 114-16
Iliad, see Homer
imitation, 110 (*see also mimesis*)
imperial system, historians' reflections on, 82-3, 85-6, 90-106, 116, 118-19
individuals, de-emphasised, 31, 37-8, 64-5
innuendo, Tacitus master of, 98-101
inscriptions, 32, 82, 92, 101
inventio, see elaboration
Ionia, *see* Asia Minor
Ionian
    dialect, 15
    Revolt, 13, 19
    science, 16, 18
Isokrates, 46, 48

Jacoby, F., 39, 46, 127
Janus, temple of, 79
Jerome, 94
Jews, the, 117
Josephus, 117
Jugurtha, 65, 67, 69-70
Julio-Claudians, 80, 90-1, 96
Jupiter Feretrius, temple of, 82-3

Kallisthenes, 52
Kerkyra (Corfu), 29, 35, 68
Kimon, 77
Kleitos, 116
Kleon, 32

lacunas, 44
Leuktra, battle of, 41-2
Lives, *see* biographical focus
Livy
    life and works, 60-1, **79-89**, 90-1, 97, 118
    structure of his history, 81-2, 85-6, 88
local history, 61, 64
loss of most ancient historians, 39,

44, 46, 49, 55-7, 60, 62-3, 65,
    71, 76, 79-81, 91, 93-6,
    118-19, 122 (*see also*
    fragments)
Lucceius, friend of Cicero, 67, 71
Lucretia (wife of Collatinus), 86-7
Lydian Empire, 18-19, 23
Lyons, 101

Macedonia, 46-7, 51, 55, 57-8, 111
    (*see also* Alexander the Great,
    Philip II, Philip V)
Mantineia, battle of (362 BC), 41
Mantineia, sack of (223 BC), 55-6
Mardonios, 24
Marius, 65-6, 70, 112, 118
medicine, language of, 30
megalomania, 21-2, 111, 113
Melos, Melian Dialogue, 35-6, 43
memoirs, 39-40, 74-5
Messenia, 42
methodology, 16-18, 26-8, 31, 48, 55,
    104, 109-10 and *passim* (*see
    also* prefaces and prologues)
metus hostilis, 85
mimesis (dramatic presentation), 55
miracles, *see* wonders and marvels
'mirror of Herodotos', 19-21, 93
mixed constitution, 60
modern history, difference from
    ancient, 12, 24, 122
monarchy, 20, 79, 86-7, 90-106, 116,
    118-19
monograph, 67
moral lessons in history, 12, 18, 21-4,
    37-8, 43-4, 46, 73, 82, 86-9,
    101, 109-12, 122
morality, erosion of, 34-6, 66-70,
    83-5, 93
Mykale, Battle of, 13, 77
myth, rationalising approach to,
    16-17, 24, 84

Naevius, 63
names, Roman, 118
nationalistic focus in Roman
    historiography, 64, 82, 84
nemesis, 21-4, 35-6
Nepos, 71, **76-8**, 103

Nero, 90, 96, 105-6
Nerva, 90-1, 93
'new men' (*novi homines*), 65-6, 68-9
Nikolaos of Damascus, 60
novel, the, 124
novi homines, see 'new men'
Numidia, *see* Jugurtha

obituaries, 100
Octavian, *see* Augustus
Odyssey, 18 (*see also* Homer,
    influence of)
Oedipus, *Oedipus Tyrannus,* 23
oligarchy, 20, 47
Olympic Games, Olympiads, 58
oral tradition, 11, 16-18
oratory, relationship with history, 33,
    47-8, 71-4, 106
'Oxyrhynchos historian', **44-6**

papyrus, 19, 44
Paris (Trojan prince), 11, 17
Parthia, 66, 113, 116
Peace of Nikias, 26, 30
Peiraieus, 30, 40
Peloponnesian War, 25-40, 44
    causes of, 28-31, 49-50
    definition of, 25-6, 30
Pelopidas, 42
pentads, *see* decades
Pentekontaetia, 29-30, 49
Perikles, 32-4, 50, 110-11
periods, periodisation, 10
Perseus of Macedon, 57, 81
Persian Empire, 13-5, 18-21, 23,
    39-40, 51, 60, 116
Persian Wars (fifth century), 13-15,
    17, 21-7, 29, 61
Persians, The (play by Aischylos),
    23
Pharsalos, battle of, 65
Philip II of Macedon, 46-7, 51
Philip V of Macedon, 57, 81
Philippi, battle of, 66
Phoenicians, 17
Phylarchos, **55-6**, 58, 74
Plataia, Battle of, 13
Plato, 40
plausibility, 31, 72-4, 98-9, 100-1

(*see also* elaboration of material)
Plutarch, 46, 52, 61, 92, **107-12**, 114, 118
political theory, 43, 60
Polybios, 46-7, 49, 55-6, **56-60**, 61, 82, 117
Pompey, 65, 74, 79, 91, 109
Pontifex Maximus, 63
Poteidaia, 29
pragmatike historia, 58-9
Pre-Socratic philosophers, 16
prefaces and prologues, 15-18, 26-8, 39, 57-8, 67-70, 77, 83-6, 94-8, 109-10, 113-14, 117-18
propaganda, 41-2, 56, 64, 75-6
provincial perspective, 91-2, 117-18
Ptolemy, Ptolemies, 51, 113-14
Punic Wars, 61, 63-4, 81, 88 (*see also* Hannibal)

Quintilian, 73-4

recent past as subject of history, 18, 28, 31, 60, 81, 84, 91, 94, 96-7, 102, 109, 112
religious dimension in history, 12, 21-4, 31, 42-3, 59-60, 63, 84, 87-9
Renaissance, 122
Republic, restoration of, 79, 84-5, 119
research, 15-18, 24, 55, 68, 82, 111
(*see also historia/historie*; oral tradition; sources)
rhetoric, *see* oratory
rivalry between historians, 15-16, 26-7, 30, 47, 53-6, 83, 96-7, 113 (*see also* Homer, influence of)
Rome
conquest of Greece, 57, 61, 64, 81, 107
explanations for its success, 56-61, 117-18
its culture explained for Greek readers, 118
sack of (390 BC), 82, 88-9
supposed Greek origin of, 61
Romulus, 109

Rubicon, crossing of, 65
sack of a city, opportunity for elaboration, 55-6, 73-4, 97
Salamis, Battle of, 14, 22-3
Sallust, **66-71**, 76, 85, 94, 86, 97
Samos, 18, 40 (*see also* Douris of Samos)
'scientific history', 31-3, 41
Scipio Aemilianus, 57
Scythia, 19-20, 48
Second Athenian Confederacy, 42
Sejanus, 99
selection of material, 24, 33-8, 46-8, 68, 101, 109-10, 112
Senate, 60, 65-70, 74, 79, 88, 90-1, 98-9, 101-3, 105-6 (*see also* aristocratic families, Roman)
sex, 47, 105-6
Sextus Tarquinius, 86-7
Sicilian Expedition, 30, 32-3, 36-7, 43
Sicily, 65 (*see also* Sicilian Expedition)
Sokrates, 39-40, 44
Solon, 22-3
Sophokles, 23, 112
sources
later historians using earlier as, 45, 49-50, 81-2, 111-14, 117
treatment of, 16-17, 24, 27-8, 31, 41, 72-4, 82
Sparta, 20-1, 25, 28-31, 34, 39-43, 47, 51
speeches
historians' treatment of, 20, 27-8, 33-4, 68-9, 73, 101, 118
destabilising reader's reactions, 68-9, 94
Strabo, 48
style, linguistic, 31, 39, 45-6, 58-9, 75-6, 95-6, 119
Suetonius, 91-2, **103-6**, 118
sufferings, emphasised by the historian, 26-8, 34-5, 36, 95, 97-8
Sulla, 65, 70, 112
synkrisis, see comparison
Syracuse, 36, 53

Tacitus, 91-2, **93-101**, 102-4, 118

Agricola, 93-4
Annals, 96-101
Histories, 94-6
Tarquinius Superbus, 86-7
Teleutias, 43-4
Thales, 16
Thebes, 41-3, 45
Theopompos of Chios, **46-8**, 55
Theramenes, 32
Thermopylai, Battle of, 13
Theseus, 109
third person, use of, 75
Thirty-Years Peace, 25, 28-9
Thrace, 19, 25
Thucydides, **25-38**, 53, 56
    accuracy of, 31-3, 46, 49-50, 73,
        101
    influence of, 39-41, 45, 58-9, 68,
        71, 86, 95, 104, 112, 119, 122
Tiberius, 90-1, 96, 98-103
Timaios, 58
tragedy and tragic sensibility, 12, 15,
    21-4, 35-6, 111
'tragic history', 53-6
Trajan, 90-1, 116-17
translations, 126-7
treason trials, 90-1, 99, 102
tribute (tax), 32
troop numbers, inflated, 82
Troy, 11, 17 (*see also* Homer,
    influence of)

'universal history', 48-9, 57-8, 60, 76

usefulness of history, 37-8, 53-5, 59,
    86, 97-8 (*see also* moral
    lessons in history)
Utica, 66

Veii, 81, 88-9
Velleius Paterculus, **102-3**
Vespasian, 90, 95
Vestal Virgins, 105-6
vividness, an aim of the historian, 53,
    73-4 (*see also* dramatic and/or
    exciting presentation)
Vulgate, *see* Alexander the Great,
    historians of

war, traditional subject of history, 12,
    14-15, 31, 41, 58, 97, 104-5,
    109-10
wise advisor, the, 23
women, their treatment by the
    historians, 12, 87, 95
wonders and marvels, subject of
    historian, 18, 47, 52

Xenokles, 45
Xenophon, **39-44**, 49-50, 59, 74-5,
    82, 112-15
Xerxes, 20-4

Year of Four Emperors, 80, 90, 94-6

Zeus, 11, 17, 22, 43 (*see also*
    religious dimension in history)